Confessions of a Civil Servant

Lessons in Changing America's Government and Military

BOB STONE

ROWMAN & LITTLEFIELD PUBLISHERS, INC.
Lanham • Boulder • New York • Toronto • Oxford

ROWMAN & LITTLEFIELD PUBLISHERS, INC.

Published in the United States of America
by Rowman & Littlefield Publishers, Inc.
A wholly owned subsidiary of The Rowman & Littlefield Publishing Group, Inc.
4501 Forbes Boulevard, Suite 200, Lanham, Maryland 20706
www.rowmanlittlefield.com

PO Box 317
Oxford
OX2 9RU, UK

British Library Cataloguing in Publication Information Available

The hardback edition of this book was previously catalogued by the Library of Congress
as follows:

Stone, Bob, 1935-
  Confessions of a civil servant : lessons in changing America's
government and military / Bob Stone.
    p. cm.
Includes index.
  1. Administrative agencies—United States—Management. 2.
Organizational change—United States. 3. United States—Armed
Forces—Management. 4. United States—Politics and government. I.
Title.
  JK421 .S746 2002
  352.3'67'0973—dc21
                                                    2002011611

ISBN 0-7425-2764-6 (hardcover : alk. paper); ISBN 0-7425-2765-4 (pbk. : alk. paper)

Printed in the United States of America

♾™ The paper used in this publication meets the minimum requirements of American
National Standard for Information Sciences—Permanence of Paper
for Printed Library Materials, ANSI/NISO Z39.48–1992.

DEDICATION

—To David Osborne, who made me famous; got me the best job a civil servant could ever have (reinventing government); then recruited me into the Public Strategies Group, the world's best group of government consultants; and, finally, persuaded me that I had this book in me.

—To my bosses in government who trusted me, who stretched my mind and heart, and who didn't try to fix me: John Ahearne, Bill Brehm, Irv Greenberg, Robin Pirie, Larry Korb, Elaine Kamarck, Morley Winograd, and Al Gore.

—To Tom Peters, who inspired me with tales of excellence in the private sector.

—To Bill Creech, who inspired and mentored me and a generation of military leaders with his decentralizing, empowering, mission-driven leadership.

—And most of all to Roxane Stern, love of my life, who believed in me, helped me, encouraged me, and made sure that I was always able to throw my heart into my work. Roxane, my heart was always with you.

Contents

Foreword

Tom Peters

"Some people look for things that went wrong and try to fix them. I look for things that went right and try to build on them."

—*Bob Stone/Mr. ReGo/Energizer-in-Chief*

* * * *

THE PARTIAL ReGo* (*Reinventing Government)
HEROES' HONOR ROLL

Jerry Bolden, AG/Gulfport, Mississippi	Sue Bruederle, FDA/Chicago
Joe Dear, OSHA HQ	Hugh Doran, VA/Kansas City
Ed Esparza, FDA/Dallas	Bill Freeman, OSHA/Maine
Lynn Gordon, U.S. Customs/Miami	Joan Hyatt, OSHA/Colorado
Mike Loh, USAF	Joe Thompson, VA/New York City
Marie Urban, FDA HQ	Bob Wenzel, IRS/Fresno

(Remember these names . . . damn it.)

* * * *

Bob Stone reinvented the Department of Defense. Not content, he then reinvented the entire Federal Government.

Well, actually, that's bull. The job's not done.

But the progress—mostly unsung—has been stupendous.

(Yes, damn it, s-t-u-p-e-n-d-o-u-s.)

Bob's business cards read "Energizer-in-Chief." Which is to say that Bob *didn't* reinvent government. But Lynn Gordon, Bill Freeman, and Bob Wenzel et al. did. (See above. See within. Their stories are *the* story.)

This is, simply, the best text ever on "making it in government." That is, getting BIG Things Done That Matter. This may also be the BTE/best text ever on large-scale organization change. Anywhere.

Here's the deal . . .

Bob Stone was a nerdy engineer, with a proclivity for solving thorny problems. And, as we old Navy types put it . . . Damn the Torpedoes (i.e., recalcitrant bosses who failed to see the light/his light) in the process.

He fixed things. He was blunt. (Most engineers are.) He was constantly in trouble. "Didn't suffer fools lightly" comes to mind.

But Bob's raw skill and sheer chutzpah finally landed him a job as Deputy Assistant Secretary of Defense for Installations. ("Bases" to civilians.)

Bob was appalled at what he found. He's genetically averse to "good enough for government work"—and believes that great bases are the cornerstone of motivated troops and defense readiness. In short, a million bits of petty B.S., ordered from on high, shouted distrust of civilians in government service—and impaired rapid, efficient common-sense practices at every turn. Readiness and troop morale were the victims of this complex, unintentional, anti-excellence conspiracy.

The Stone Way was resisted—mightily—at headquarters (The Pentagon). But Bob found real people who cared—mightily—in the field where the soldiers and sailors and airmen and marines live and work.

Bob met Bill Creech, one of my all-time "corporate" heroes. General Bill, in astonishingly short order, had turned around (turned upside down!) the massive Tactical Air Command of the U.S. Air Force (now the Air Combat Command). Creech empowered the front line, cut the crap, reinstalled pride in work sapped during the wretched, hypercentralized McNamara years . . . and arguably created the most battle-ready force in U.S. military history. (Witness TAC's performance in the Gulf War.)

General Bill reinforced Bob Stone's belief that "it" "could be done" "fast" despite Washington's micromanagement.

To make a long story short (read the book), Bob recruited Bill (or vice versa, it doesn't matter) . . . and the field-led, Bob Stone–energized campaign for more troop-friendly, high-performance bases was on with a vengeance.

Bill Creech was the model. And "model" is a (the?!) key word in this astounding saga. Bob is an avowed enemy of command and control, "gotcha" management. And a maestro of "show 'em an example of someone 'real' who's doing it right"—in spite of the same B.S. that everyone else faces. (Bob gives me some credit for this, but he ought to cite Ken Blanchard, for whom "catching someone doing something right" is axiom number one of effective change and leadership.) At Defense, Bob's showcase/s (literally) was the Model Installations Program. And Creech provided the first certified exemplar—a long way from HQ—another Stone–Creech principal tenet. (Message: good weird things rarely happen in the shadow of headquarters.)

Model Installations pissed off the Pentagon, whose Ultimate Authority Over Positively Every Small Thing it challenged—and was enthusiastically embraced by caring commanders, obsessed by readiness in the field. And the world of defense wobbled a bit on its axis.

As the years (Reagan Years) passed, Bob irritated most everyone in his hierarchy—which proved to be the right launching pad for the Main Game reported in these pages.

I remember well sitting at my desk on my farm in Vermont late one evening in 1993. The fax clattered . . . and out spooled a brief hand-written note on the stationery of the Vice President of the United States of America. "Guess who's been picked to reinvent government?" it read. Signed . . . Bob Stone.

Exaggeration? No, it turns out. Vice President Al Gore made an early decision, supported by his boss, to make the dull (or so it appeared at the time) task of "reforming government" into a moral crusade of the first order. And he chose an apparently unassuming-but-uncivil servant to do the job. (Message: In the repetitious past, a "famous" businessman was typically chosen to do "it"—and the "reform" "product" was an inflammatory report informing us that all two million government "bureaucrats" were jerks. This time Gore wisely chose an insider who fervently believed the government was loaded with "radicals" who ached to break the insipid rules, make big waves, and do a great job of serving their customers—soldiers and sailors and U.S. taxpayers.)

Through one of those "networking things" Mr. Gore encountered Mr. Stone. (Stone admits that "learning" networking didn't come easily for a reluctant, just-the-facts engineer . . . but master the art he did. And he commands all would-be change impresarios to do the same. TP1: Right on, Bro. Stone. TP2: Networking = Suck up, build and mind your Rolodex = Absolute Essential for those who want to Make a Difference in large systems.)

Bob got his Moment-in-the-Big Office. He was the consummate "briefer" by now. Not the typical engineer-bureaucrat-consultant's slide-after-slide awash in eight-point-type numbers. But story after story after story of hero after hero after hero . . . illustrated with physical props that graphically revealed the silliness of life-in-government for those determined, against all odds, to make things better for their "Customers" (whoops . . . the "dirty" C-word . . . see below).

Bob got the job! The Dream Job. Only one thing left . . . make it happen. Fast. He was painfully aware of the dusty fate of most "Commission Reports" on "good government." The war against excess paperwork usually resulted in . . . more unread paper.

So Bob and his merry band of battle-scarred reprobates from all across government took a diametrically opposite approach, reminiscent on a large scale of his DOD effort. And that approach is the cornerstone of this magisterial book. Stone & Co. chose not to pontificate and analyze. They chose not to hire a battalion of consultants. (Beltway Bandits, as they're all too appropriately called.) Instead, they sought Heroes. Within. He sought out what Nancy Austin and I, in *A Passion for Excellence*, called "pockets of excellence." Those daring souls who had already chosen, against the odds and at risk of their jobs (yes, even the civil service), to follow the True Path of Public Service ... and Make a Damn Difference by Providing Excellence Directly to Their Customers.

Thus the unearthing—and boisterous celebration—of those whose names led off this Foreword. Lynn Gordon, Bill Freeman, et (many, many) al.

Some important Executive Orders were written along the way, but it turns out mostly that we didn't need to reinvent government. We needed instead to recognize the heroes within—and do anything and everything to make their way the new way. Which often meant just getting out of their way.* Celebrating their successes with megaphones in hand. Urging others to walk-trot-sprint down this same path to excellence ... bullet wounds for pioneers not withstanding.

Peter Drucker: "Ninety percent of what we call 'management' consists of making it difficult to get things done." (And PD was talking private sector!)

Management and change are my bailiwicks. Such work has traditionally been tuned into The Plan ... The Processes ... The Edicts from On Holy High. Bob Stone turns that conventional wisdom on its head. And I say ... Hooray! Long overdue! (Private and public sector.)

PowerPoint slides are the staple of my one hundred seminars per year. I tried to capture Bob's "Grand New Change Message" on just one slide. I ignored his "rule of three" (sorry, Bob) . . . and offer my *12 Lessons in Stone* instead. To wit:

1. **Demos and Models.** "Model Installations." (DOD.) "ReGo Labs." (Reinventing government laboratories.) In any event the idea is that we learn . . . by example. Period. "Go there." "Look." "Do your own version, but understand that we have some Concrete Exemplars of the New Way . . . performed by people like yourself."

2. **Heroes.** An obvious extension of the above. Consider the folks the president puts in the House Gallery during the State of the Union address. These heroes are the living embodiment of folks "just like us" who have made a damn difference—relative to topics central to POTUS's strategic agenda.

3. **Stories and Storytellers.** Several prominent students of leadership, notably Harvard's Howard Gardner, have argued that stories are the leader's . . . *most potent tool.* I'd add . . . AMEN. Such stories take on added potency when there are—à la Bob Stone—leave-behind props that illustrate graphically the Main Point. Addendum: There were . . . and are . . . Great Storytellers. Effective leaders need a Garrison Keillor gene, perhaps. (Or they can learn it—again, see Formerly Nerdy Stone.)

4. **Chroniclers.** *We need the Hard Evidence.* Bob did a masterful job of spreading The Stories . . .via world-class videography, pamphlets, and the like. If it's not solidly chronicled . . . then it never was!

5. **Cheerleaders and Recognition.** As always, positive reinforcement remains the most powerful "device" known to man. Bob Stone was a badges and buttons and baubles fanatic in a world where praise is sparing. (Understatement.) (Hey, Mary Kay had nothing on the ReGo troops when it came to r-e-c-o-g-n-i-t-i-o-n.)

6. **New Language.** Winston Churchill famously said, "We shape our buildings and then they shape us." So, too, words. Bob Stone's insistence on using the word "customer" was mocked by some—but made an enormous difference over the course of time. In general, he changed the vocabulary of public service from *"procedure first"* to *"service first."* From *"HQ boss first"* to *"field service provider first."* From *"distrust"* to *"trust"* (of the service-delivery team). From *"adversary"* aiming to *"score"* at the customer's expense to *"partner"* aiming to *"get the right things done."* And so on. A very big deal!

7. **Seekers.** Finding the New Heroes is not necessarily a walk in the park—they've been working to stay beneath the radar scope for years; hence, a/the primary mission of ReGo staffers is to ferret them out.

8. **Protectors.** Some of Bob's New Heroes didn't want the publicity—they were already at odds with their bureaucracies. Hence, staffers must protect those they discover. (Face time with Vice President Gore kept a few of Stone's Heroes from losing their jobs—hard to fire someone who just pocketed an Award of Valor from the Vice President of the United States in front of the press!)

9. **Support Groups.** Pioneers need pals—like-minded souls to commiserate with and learn from (new tricks for beating the system and avoiding capture). ReGo events and networking practices helped here. Lots.

10. **End Runs/Pull Strategy.** This is less a ReGo strategy than a corporate strategy I've observed among change masters. Forget changing recalcitrant insiders; hook up with oddball customers and vendors who end up pulling the enterprise, kicking and screaming if necessary, into the future. In a way, of course, this was the Whole Deal for Stone & Co.

11. **Field/"Real People" Focus.** At DOD, Stone started a revolution—among concerned base commanders . . . a long way from home. "Headquarters revolution" is by and large an oxymoron!

12. **Speed.** Move fast, Stone counsels . . . before the forces of evil have a chance to kill you by memo and endless reviews. Former Air Force Colonel John Boyd said whoever has the fastest O.O.D.A. Loops wins (O.O.D.A. Loop = Observe-Orient-Decide-Act Cycle). Confuse and confound the enemy by your speed per se: he's busy scheduling the review . . . as you finish the job.

The above, I believe, captures the outlines of a most remarkable transformation executed by Bob Stone and a small and remarkable band of True Patriots—aiming to allow those closest to the scene to serve their customers with vigor, imagination, and efficiency. As I said at the outset, the job is not done . . . by a long shot. But perhaps the process is close to irreversible. Public Servants who care have been exposed to a taste of excellence and empowerment. They are not likely to soon lose their appetites.

Bob et al. found the best of the best and paraded them before the Vice President, their compatriots, and, as often as possible, the citizenry. These new exemplars offered heart and hope to others. While not all public servants have the pioneering spirit, Bob Stone and I believe that the great majority would rather do a good job than a bad job. A well-intentioned system of government checks and balances run amok has often kept them from doing so. "By the book" has become synonymous with delay and obfuscation ... and downright disregard and contempt for the "customer" (soldier, sailor, taxpayer).

Bob Stone has a lovely array of commendations in his quiver. But each one is matched—times ten—by barbs and arrows shot at him. Yet he has persevered. He believes in the basic tenets of Public Service. And he has made an enormous contribution. By taking the time to share his extraordinary experiences with readers in the private as well as public sector, he has done us all one more great service.

Thanks, Bob!

Tom Peters/19 May 2002/West Tisbury, MA

Preface to the Paperback Edition

I've been on a perpetual book tour of sorts since the hardcover edition came out a year ago—a book tour not to sell books, but ideas, and to engage hearts and minds over public service. So I spend my time mostly doing two things: lecturing to students and doing workshops for government leaders at all levels.

I've been delighted by my reception. Students of public administration are hungry to learn about public service. They are leaning toward public service because they want to do important things, but they're not sure. They're full of questions:

- Is government just too bureaucratic for a person to get things done?
- Do I have to wait years to make a contribution?
- Can I say what I think?

And the big question:

- Can I make a difference?

I've been able to reassure them on all these questions, and have left all of my sessions more convinced than before of the need for this book, and of its utility in the classroom.

The hardcover edition is already being used as a text at several universities. Here are reactions from a few of the professors using *Confessions of a Civil Servant* in their courses:

"My students are enjoying this book so much I have decided to use it again next semester."—**Veronica Cruz, SUNY-Albany**

"This book richly depicts Bob Stone's experiences in public service. Stone's passion for innovation and positive change in government and his courageous and caring leadership are evident throughout the book. My students raved about this book!"—Gary S. Marshall, University of Nebraska, Omaha

"What it's really like to be a civil servant and to try and create change in the bureaucracy. It is a wonderful read and filled with important lessons for anyone in any big organization."—Elaine Kamarck, John F. Kennedy School of Government, Harvard University

Taken as a whole, the book gives a rich picture of one person's thirty-year journey in government service. It describes successes, failures, mistakes, and "learnings;" and most important, the possibilities of making a difference.

But, taken chapter by chapter, the book can be the basis for classroom discussions or essays that get students deeply engaged and teaching themselves. At the end of each chapter, its themes are repeated and are followed by its lessons. By getting students to discuss these themes and lessons, the teacher can help the students get the most out of the book and learn many of the most important issues in public administration.

Where to start depends on the subject matter of the course. For example, if the subject is government regulation, chapters 2 ("Shrinking Regulations") and 11 ("Strengthening the Regulatory Process") would be highly relevant. If the subject is innovation, then chapters 9 ("Encouraging and Protecting Innovators") and 14 ("Getting Past the Barriers to Change") would be relevant. A review of the table of contents will give the reader more ideas.

But what government needs most is *better bosses*! The most important lesson in the book is that public service requires leadership, and leadership can be taught. That's why chapter 15 ("Ten Lessons in Leadership") is the most important chapter. I've conducted dozens of lectures and workshops for government leaders built around this chapter. These workshops have been the most exciting and rewarding experiences of all. Participants have been fully engaged and hungry for insights into how they might become better leaders in public service.

Mid-career public servants and senior executives are most in need of—and most receptive to—the lessons in leadership because, I believe, they have been most subjected to bad leadership during their careers. A study of chapter 15 can help in two ways: it can turn around people who have learned and practiced the old Theory X management style, and it can increase the confidence of people who want to be a different kind of leader but fear that their style is not the most effective way to lead. *It is!*

If students of public administration and people already in government learn nothing more than the lessons of chapter 15, they will be far better prepared for public service than I was.

Acknowledgments

My partners at the Public Strategies Group encouraged me in my writing even as I disappeared from view. They actually paid me while I was writing—not consulting. Babak Armajani and Peter Hutchinson especially kept assuring me that the company was getting its money's worth, even when I wasn't so sure.

Birgitta Gregory, my coach, helped me figure out that the book was my top priority and extracted from me a schedule for completion. My accountability to Birgitta made it easy to keep to the schedule.

Many of my friends and former colleagues read parts of the material, provided useful comments, and corrected many errors and omissions. Thanks to Camille Barnett, Bill Creech, John Fallon, Irv Greenberg, John Kamensky, Gerry Kauvar, David Osborne, George Schlossberg, Chris Tirpak, Joe Thompson, Marie Urban, and Greg Woods.

Everyone wants to be a hero to one's family, so thanks to my kids—Sue Le, Rob Stone, Marc Stern, and Lisa Stern—who read parts of the book and thought it was *sensational!*

Nita Young and Sue Willett read parts of the book and said they found it fascinating. Since they never worked for the government, their opinions carried special weight with me, even though—or especially because—they're my friends.

I'm sure I've made mistakes in spite of the best efforts of all those who tried to help me get it all straight. All the mistakes belong to me exclusively.

Roxane Stern has been my best and toughest critic. She read every word and made countless suggestions for improvement.

Of course, my greatest debt is to the federal employees who lived the stories that I've told. They get out the checks, collect the taxes, keep us safe, preserve the union, and do a heck of a job. They deserve the admiration of all Americans. I hope this book helps them get it.

Introduction
On Government Service

In 1969, I left my job as an engineer with Garrett-AiResearch Manufacturing Company in Los Angeles to go to work for the Department of Defense (DOD). I loved my job at Garrett, but the opportunity to work at the Pentagon and perhaps make a difference to the war effort drew me to Washington. I was so sure I'd be back in two or three years that I kept my season tickets to the Los Angeles Rams.

I stayed thirty years.

I learned to marvel at the remarkable people who make our government work. I was especially filled with wonder at the soldiers, sailors, marines, and airmen who defend America, and their wives or husbands who keep their families going during deployment, overseas stationing, exercises, and war.

I learned to abhor the systems of bureaucracy—the centralization and over-regulation—that undervalue all these public servants and keep them from contributing all they can. I fought to decentralize and deregulate the bureaucracy to free them to serve America better.

This book is about both the bureaucracy and the greatness I ran into, and about how leaders can move their organizations from one to the other. The methods—decentralization, deregulation, devolution of authority in a value-centered organization—are applicable to any large enterprise—local government, federal government, the military, or business. My own passion and experience center on government and the military, and it's here that I believe so strongly that the move to greatness is perfectly possible and pressing.

The American people haven't always appreciated what they had in their government. Some politicians decried government as the source of our problems. More called public servants "bureaucrats," and distrusted and insulted them. Most Americans simply took government for granted.

Then came the horrific events of September 11, 2001. Suddenly Americans woke up to the realization that government matters. We need it to be extraordinarily more effective in policing our borders. We need it to mobilize the nation's defenses against terror at home. And we need it to become much more efficient because the war on terrorism is so expensive and is sapping resources from other government functions.

To become more effective and more efficient, government at all levels—city, county, state, and federal—must transform itself from a middling-performing bureaucracy to a top-notch, twenty-first century, high-performing organization. The workers are perfectly capable. To paraphrase *My Fair Lady*'s Alfred P. Doolittle, they're willing to do it, they're wanting to do it, they're waiting to do it. All they need is the right leadership. The times demand it.

I hope this book can help government leaders—civil servants, military, and political appointees—to provide that leadership.

1

Brazen Chariots, Brazen Analysts

(Tackling a Job When
You Haven't a Clue)

"Ivan, this is Bob. I'm all packed, leaving in the morning on American, Flight 61. It's scheduled to arrive at Dulles at 4:45 P.M."

Ivan was Ivan Selin, recent McNamara whiz kid, chosen just six weeks earlier, in March 1969, by new Secretary of Defense Melvin Laird to be the Assistant Secretary of Defense for Systems Analysis. One of the early things Ivan had done after being named was to invite me to fly to Washington from Los Angeles for an interview. The interview had gone wonderfully, and I was headed to Washington to start work in the Pentagon. I was filled with excitement and awe.

I had no experience in systems analysis, or in government, for that matter. I had spent most of my eleven years since college as a heat transfer engineer in the aerospace industry. I usually was assigned to analyze ill-defined problems where nobody really knew what the problem was, let alone the solution. For the last year I had been trying to market—without success—a cooler I had designed for exhaust ducts of Army helicopters to protect them from heat-seeking missiles. So I did know a little—very little—about helicopters. And Ivan had told me he would ease my start in the Pentagon by putting me to work analyzing the Army helicopter program.

"That's great, Bob. I'll have my driver pick you up and bring you to the house. Hey, do you know anything about tanks? Turns out, I really need you to look over the Army tank program. Helicopters are in pretty good shape, but there are big problems with the Army over tank procurement."

My heart sank. I had been counting on starting work on something familiar, and the papers were filled every day with stories of helicopter exploits in the Vietnam War, then, in the spring of 1969, at its peak. After all, I *had* assembled a toy model of an Army "Huey" helicopter as an aid to my analysis at work.

"No, actually I don't know a thing about tanks, but I guess I could learn."

"That's great. See you tomorrow."

Next morning I made a point of getting to the airport early, so I'd have a chance to shop at the newsstand for something that would teach me about tanks. I headed right for the paperback section, to the rotating bookcase with the big sign on top: BALLANTINE BOOKS' HISTORY OF WORLD WAR II.

Let's see, *The Battle of Midway*? Nope, I was certain that tanks hadn't even been present at Midway—only aircraft carriers, battleships, and airplanes. Ditto for *Pearl Harbor* and *The Battle of Britain*. And then, suddenly . . . there it was!

Brazen Chariots, by Major Robert Crisp. "The finest narrative of tank warfare to come out of World War II."—*Los Angeles Times*. "Belongs in the first rank of combat books..."—*Time Magazine*.

That was it! I would read *Brazen Chariots* on the plane to D.C. and would learn all about tanks—or enough to start work.

The next day I reported to the Office of the Secretary of Defense (OSD), ready to analyze the Army's most important programs, a new family of tanks and antitank missiles that were far more complicated, more expensive, and potentially more lethal than anything that had come before.

My credentials? A master's degree in chemical engineering from the Massachusetts Institute of Technology (MIT), eleven years designing heat exchangers for airplanes and spacecraft, and four hours reading *Brazen Chariots*.

My colleagues on the Office of the Secretary of Defense staff? A couple of brilliant junior military officers serving as analysts—their credentials, the Army ROTC course; and a few civilians with no military service at all—like me.

My adversaries? Led by William Westmoreland, Bruce Palmer, and Bill DePuy, Army chief of staff, vice chief, and assistant vice chief, respectively, they included super-bright colonels and lieutenant colonels on the Army staff, many of whom later rose to the very top rank: four-star general. Their credentials? Most had four years at West Point, all had served in real combat, and some had even fought tank battles in World War II.

They weren't really adversaries, of course. They were trying to defend the Army's interests against a bunch of kids (I was the old man of the OSD team at age thirty-four) who had never been near combat and had barely solved any problems except in college.

They worked hard to educate my buddies and me. Colin Powell, then a lieutenant colonel, introduced himself as our babysitter. His assignment was to make sure we didn't cause any real trouble for the Army. He sat around and told hilarious stories about his service in Vietnam and patiently explained to us when and how we had blundered in our analytical assumptions or in our relationships with our "betters" (the Army staff).

I was soon introduced to the military's great attention to detail and to rank. One day the Army was to brief Paul Bowron (a GS-18, the highest civil service rank at that time), me (a GS-15), and two junior staffers, Patrick Gross (GS-13) and Charlie Atkins (GS-12). When we arrived in the briefing room, there were name cards at our places, like so:

| Mr. Gross | Mr. Bowron | Mr. Stone | Mr. Atkins |

After a while we broke for lunch, and Bowron went off to do something else, leaving just three of us to be briefed. Sure enough, when we returned from lunch the name cards had been rearranged, keeping the ranking person nearest the center and the next ranking person to his right, in accordance with military protocol:

| Mr. Atkins | Mr. Stone | Mr. Gross |

It was my first lesson in the DOD culture of rank—part courtesy, part tradition, and part organizational rigidity—necessary in war but curious to a newcomer like me.

I soon ran into far more curious behavior, imposed by OSD under Secretary Robert McNamara, that involved a huge waste of human talent. OSD had centralized all authority for planning—down to the smallest details of weapon procurement—and required the military to submit mindless justification every time a change, no matter how small, was made to the five-year defense program (FYDP). There were thousands of changes that required OSD approval. One year the Army adjusted its planned buy of Shillelagh missiles down, from about 57,000 to 55,000. The change was accompanied by a one-inch thick "Program Change Request."

In those days before word processors, such a package would have taken several staff days to prepare (not counting the substantive analysis that may have gone into it). It fell to me to decide whether to approve this piddling change in the totally unknowable five-year program (we were at war in Vietnam at the time), and I took all of one minute to approve it.

There were, however, greater wastes of human talent. The Joint Chiefs of Staff (JCS) produced, also at the direction of OSD, a monumental annual work called the *Joint Strategic Objectives Plan* (*JSOP*), which filled an entire file cabinet. I was in the Land Forces office, so I set about to read Volume Four, Books 1–4, *Land Forces*. When I found absolutely nothing in its 800 pages of any value to me in my work, I asked around and learned that I was the only customer for Volume Four.

I called the JCS and went to see the colonel whose job it was to produce it. I told him that I had learned that I was the only customer, and, moreover, I was apparently the only person who had ever opened the book—so he could just stop doing it and turn his efforts, and those of his four- or five-person office, to more useful pursuits. But nothing could be done based on my say-so, so the JCS continued to turn out this useless piece of work, still officially demanded by OSD, for several more years.

The *JSOP* wasn't any help to me in my principal task—figuring out how big the Army should be after Vietnam. The resources of the Pentagon, including such brilliant officers as Colin Powell, Maxwell Thurman, Glenn Otis, and Joseph Palastra, were at my disposal to help get the answers needed to solve this big issue.

When we asked questions of these officers (brazen as I was, even then I knew that these remarkable men knew far more than I about war), we got answers. For example, I soon discovered that Army forces contained lots of cannons and howitzers that fired lots of ammunition, but I couldn't envision their doing any serious damage to Soviet tank forces, their presumptive enemy.

"How come the Army has so much artillery?" I asked Lieutenant Colonel Robert "Bob" Schneider, one of my Army handlers and a career artillery officer. I didn't realize it when I spoke, but that was a very threatening question to an artillery officer.

It was one of the first of my naïve questions at the Pentagon. Naïve questions have a lot of power. Whenever I asked one, people treated me like Peter

Sellers in *Being There*: they were certain I was ignorant or brilliant, but they weren't sure which.

Bob Schneider knew one thing for sure: I needed education, and quick, on the importance of artillery—the "queen of the battlefield."

"It's impossible to explain simply," he told me. "You need to spend two weeks at Fort Sill, Oklahoma, the artillery school. They'll teach you its importance."

"Two weeks!" I protested. "I don't have two weeks to spend on this. Try two days."

"Can't be done," Bob stated flatly. But I held my ground, and soon I was on a plane for Oklahoma for a one and one-half day course in the glories of artillery. Bob was my official escort and mentor, and I was accompanied by Lieutenant Dan Gulling and Greg Woods. One of my first—and best—acts at the Pentagon had been to recruit Greg to work with me. I had worked with him at the Garrett Corporation, my previous job. Greg was twenty-seven at the time. He knew as little as I about land warfare but was at least as smart as I, and even more brazen. We got our fill of briefings the first day, and by the morning break the next day, we were ready for a change. As I sipped my coffee outside the classroom building, I noticed the grandstand across the road. It was filling with people. Flags were flying, and a military band was playing.

"What's going on?" I asked a soldier walking by.

"Some big shots are here, and there's a big show today."

I soon learned that we were the big shots, and the show was what the Army calls a "firepower demonstration." We took our seats in the first row and protected our ears as best we could as the soldiers brought in every howitzer, mortar, cannon, and missile they could get their hands on and shot up a storm. Or a firestorm.

At the end the announcement came over the PA, "Our distinguished guest of honor, Mr. Stone, will now fire an Honest John missile."

"NO!!" Dan Gulling expelled. "The Honest Johns cost $65,000 apiece. You can't do it."

But what could I do? The announcement had already been made to half the base plus a few thousand visitors from the nearby town of Lawton. I couldn't embarrass my hosts, so I strode out to the field, was shown by a soldier what button to push, and off went the rocket in a blaze of flame and thunder toward a simulated nuclear destruction of Tulsa, sixty miles away. After a minute or so, a giant mushroom cloud blossomed behind the hills, and the firepower demonstration was over.

"How could you do it?" Dan accused. "How could you burn up $65,000 just like that?"

I explained that the Honest John was an old missile and that the Army needed to fire one every once in a while to test its reliability. But I never knew for sure whether the firing was to test the missile or to impress me.

Now I knew about artillery, to go along with my knowledge of tanks. Greg Woods and I set off to tackle the big issue facing the nation regarding the Army: how big should the Army be?

The Army's argument was simple. Its mission was, in conjunction with our North Atlantic Treaty Organization (NATO) allies, to deter, and if necessary to defend against, an unstoppable Soviet-led Warsaw Pact invasion of Western Europe. The Soviets had 108 divisions; their Pact allies had another fifty-four, our allies had thirty. Therefore, the U.S. Army needed not less than sixteen. They never could explain very well why sixteen divisions were needed if the Warsaw Pact had enough power for an overwhelming victory anyway.

The Army had a computer model called ATLAS that simulated a hypothetical war in Central Europe. They assured us that it was very sophisticated and complicated. My boss, Paul Bowron, director of Land Forces Programs, told us Bowron's law of simulations:

Fuckedupedness = (a constant) $\times$ (complicatedness)^2

Greg and I started to dig into the model. We discovered that it operated on inputs that included number and types of weapons, firing rate in rounds per day, and lethality of each weapon against each type of target. Artillery had infinitely more lethality (defined as the area over which a very high percentage of unshielded people will be killed by the exploding round) than infantry or tanks (the simulation had been created by artillery officers) so it was the only weapon that contributed materially to the battle. When you took everything into account and multiplied all the factors together, it turned out that everything canceled out of the equation except for two variables—the total power of an Army was simply:

Power = (a constant) $\times$ (tons of artillery ammunition fired) $\times$ (lethal area per ton)

American and allied forces had known, and thus limited, supplies of ammunition. The Pact was assumed to have an infinite supply. So the Pact won all the simulations.

When we discovered how crazy the model was, we went to visit the Army's think tank, the Research Analysis Corporation,[1] where we met Abe Rosenfeld, a grizzled veteran of wars both real and analytical.

"So you think you can make the ATLAS model better?" he asked, rather threateningly.

"Yes," I answered, somewhat apprehensively. "Why don't you try something really difficult?" he responded. "Why don't you try to make it worse? Now there would be a challenge."

Whew! It was a relief and a confidence booster to know that one of the respected old hands in war gaming had as little regard for the model as we did.

Now we needed to tackle the real challenge of weighing the value of weapons and logistics on the two sides. The Pact had many more tanks than NATO, but on average they were older and less capable. It had many more artillery pieces, but NATO had more lethal ammunition. The Pact had many more divisions than NATO, but the divisions were much smaller and the reliability of the Soviet allies (e.g., Poland, Czechoslovakia, and East Germany) seemed much less than ours—mainly West Germany and Britain.

I was not ever going to trust any model that spit out an answer based on calculations that no human being could follow. I was convinced that a much better way was to apply military judgments to the pieces of the analysis, then to add them up. This was a poor method, to be sure, but I was pretty sure that all other methods were worse, in accordance with Bowron's law.

At our request, the Army convened a panel of officers to make judgments about the relative value of weapons and their value when aggregated into military units. We set the value of a single mechanized infantryman as one; then the panel judgments determined that a 155-millimeter howitzer was 100, an M60A1 tank was 140, and so on.

The panel judgments made more sense to me—and more to the point, to experienced Army people—than the firepower scores, which held a howitzer to be the equivalent of 16,000 infantry soldiers.

It remained to name our method of applying judgments to military weapon values. Greg and I wanted to call it the military judgment method. Some of our colleagues said it was simply the time-honored "Delphi method." But Bob Schneider insisted it must have an acronym.

"If you guys won't name it, the Army will."

But we refused to play that silly game, and the Army got back at us a little for discrediting and replacing the good ol' ATLAS model. They dubbed our method the Weapon Effect Indicators/Weighted Unit Value method (WEI/WUV, pronounced "wee wuv," like Elmer Fudd). And they repeated "wee wuv" with relish, always being careful to give full credit to OSD.

Nevertheless, the method made sense to everybody, and having successfully collaborated, OSD and the Army proceeded jointly to tackle the problem of assessing the total capabilities of the two sides. The Pact's 162 divisions were adjusted down in theoretical power because of their smaller size, the obviously lesser reliability of Soviet "allies," and the relatively primitive state of supporting elements of Pact forces. For example, the Pact was so short of trucks to carry troops and supplies that the Leningrad bus company had to be mobilized to carry local Soviet troops to the front lines several hundred miles to the west.

When the analysis was done, it showed the Warsaw Pact's conventional forces to be stronger than NATO's, but by a far smaller margin than previously believed. And the disparity appeared fixable if NATO undertook some relatively modest improvements, which it accomplished under the leadership of Harold Brown, Caspar Weinberger, and Frank Carlucci (defense secretaries under Presidents Carter and Reagan), along with their counterparts in West Germany and the United Kingdom.

Like many Washingtonians, I felt especially successful when the *Washington Post* said so. It was with a feeling of great accomplishment and pride when, in May 1975, I opened the morning paper and saw the headline on page one: "Study Says NATO Can Defend Itself." It seemed a long way from my days designing heat exchangers.

LESSONS FROM CHAPTER ONE:
TACKLING A JOB WHEN YOU HAVEN'T A CLUE

—Get a clue; I got one by reading *Brazen Chariots*.

—Find people who know a lot; I found Colin Powell, Bob Schneider, and others.

—Ask naïve questions; I asked why? What's that mean? Says who?

NOTE

1. Now the General Research Corporation.

A Little Yellow Book

(Shrinking Regulations)

"Larry, you have to stand up to the Army on this. They're determined to waste money. They were told by the Senate Armed Services Committee to build 300 apartments at Fort Benning for entry-level soldiers, and they're determined to build all two-bedroom units. But only half of the soldiers have kids; they could get along fine with one bedroom."

"Here's a memo to the Army for you to sign. It tells them to build half of the units with one bedroom, and it'll save $65,000."

The speaker was Perry Fliakas, Deputy Assistant Secretary of Defense for Installations and Housing.

Larry was Larry Korb, nominated just days earlier by President Reagan to be Assistant Secretary of Defense for Manpower, Reserve Affairs, and Logistics. He had no authority to sign any orders, as he was on the payroll only as a consultant. But I could sign any orders that needed to be signed, since I was acting as assistant secretary until Larry could be confirmed by the Senate.

"OK, OK. Bob'll sign it tomorrow," Larry promised.

That night I lost a lot of sleep. I wanted to accommodate my new boss, and I didn't want to force him to renege on his first commitment after his nomination, but I just couldn't bring myself to sign the order Fliakas had prepared. Next morning I garnered my courage and told Larry I couldn't sign the order.

"Perry's got it wrong. It's true that only half the junior soldiers have kids. Most of them arrive at Fort Benning without children, but most have children by the time they leave three years later. So it makes more sense for the Army to assign all the married soldiers to two-bedroom apartments rather than assigning them all to one-bedroom apartments when they show up and moving them to bigger quarters when their children are born. Anyway there's only $65,000 at stake, and I don't think we should go to the war with the Army for $65,000."

Larry grinned sheepishly. "I only said you would sign the order so I could end the conversation. But I agree it's not the right thing to do."

Two months later Larry called me in.

"I'd like to move you to the installations and housing job. Fliakas is retiring."

"I'm really happy where I am. I have a great team, I love what I'm doing, and I'd really prefer to stay put."

That's how blind I was to the opportunity I was being offered. This new job would open my eyes to the real world of defense—the bases where people were working to prepare for war, rather than the Pentagon. It would lead me to a new world of entrepreneurship and inspirational leadership; it would give me a chance to make a huge difference in the lives of millions, and it would lead to an impossible dream—working closely with the vice president to reinvent government.

But all I saw was a move from the security of a job I was very good at into the unknown. And I feared the unknown.

Larry persisted.

"I really, really want you to take the installations job."

I got the message: apparently I had no choice.

"It would be an honor. Thank you. Can I take Doug Farbrother with me?" Nobody should have to travel into the unknown without a trusted sidekick, and Doug was mine.

And off I went to be Deputy Assistant Secretary of Defense for Installations and Housing, with Doug as staff director.

The first thing I did was meet with the Navy over a problem that Congressman Roy Dyson had with a housing project at the Patuxent River Naval Air Station in Maryland. The Navy had brought some people in to meet with Fliakas. I agreed to meet with them.

Six people filed into my office, one juggling an armful of rolled-up construction drawings—I assumed of the housing project. She dropped them all on my huge conference table and started to unroll one.

I reacted quickly.

"Hey, just a minute. I have a rule: nobody unrolls drawings in my office."

It wasn't that I was afraid of drawings, although I always had a hard time figuring them out. But I was certain that any decision that depended on studying drawings should *not* be made in OSD.

That same day I met with the directors in my new organization—an admiral and four civilian senior executives. I was open with them about not knowing what they did and asked them to keep doing business as usual while I learned. My experiences with Fliakas over Fort Benning housing and with the Navy over Patuxent River housing had already convinced me that we needed a major decentralization of authority. I told the directors to start systematically to devolve lots of detailed decisions—like anything that depended on review of construction drawings—to the military departments.

"What about signature authority?" asked John Rollence, the most senior of the group and a real pro, as I was to learn.

That seemed like an easy question.

"Just keep on the road you're on. If you would have sent a paper to Fliakas to sign, well, send it to me. If you would have signed it yourself under Fliakas, go ahead and sign it now that you're reporting to me."

I was pleased with the wisdom I thought I had shown, but my response was met with stony silence.

Finally, Rollence spoke up.

"We don't have *any* signature authority. *Everything* had to go to Fliakas to sign."

I made another quick decision.

"Use your judgment. If you think I should sign it, send it to me. If you think it's a smaller matter that doesn't warrant my time, then go ahead and sign it yourself, and send me a copy."

This may have been the right decision for the long run, but in the short run, not so good. Within a day, one of the directors signed an especially arrogant memo to the military departments; I rescinded his signature authority. A few days later another director signed a memo that appeared crazy on its face.

It ordered the military departments to remove all window air conditioners on the island of Oahu in Hawaii, where all four services had huge bases. Built-in units were to be disabled by removing their compressors. The only exceptions were for an all-service housing development in Aliamanu Crater, an extinct volcano whose center was shielded from the sea breezes that, I was assured, cooled the rest of the island quite nicely.

The memo responded to complaints from the General Accounting Office (GAO) and the DOD inspector general (IG) that we were wasting money by air-conditioning houses and apartments that didn't need it—thanks to those wonderful cool sea breezes.

I was alarmed, then skeptical, even after Doug Farbrother assured me that it was an OK thing to do. Fortunately, I soon traveled to Oahu as part of a tour of our Pacific bases. A Navy captain, my escort for the trip, met me at the airport.

"Sir, do you have anything to do with air-conditioning?" he asked.

"Nnnnng," I equivocated. "Why do you ask?"

"My wife heard a rumor that they were going to disable our central air-conditioning unit, and she got real mad. She says she's stuck with me as a Navy wife through thick and thin for twenty-five years, but if they take away our air conditioner, she's through."

When I got back from the trip, I wrote a trip report about other things I had seen:

> Peculiar things are done in the field in response to pressures from Washington. For example, people ordered to save energy will do so, even if it means turning off the heat in a barracks on a very cold day or replacing bright lights with very dim lights in a maintenance hangar where people inspect high performance aircraft engines for cracks.

"Peculiar things" somehow kept being thrust at me and were to become a leitmotif of my Pentagon career. A peculiar thing called a steam trap eventually brought me some fame and landed me the dreamiest of dream jobs: working with the vice president to fix the peculiar things. But that would be a while.

My next trip was to Georgia to give a speech to a meeting of Army engineers. The military culture was never to take a chance on a big shot getting lost. A deputy assistant secretary of defense—or a general—would not be trusted to proceed alone from the Atlanta airport to a hotel. It was a matter of military courtesy. My escort was a young Army captain.

"Sir, do you have anything to do with energy conservation?"

This time I owned up.

"Yes. Why do you ask?"

"Well, sir, I live at Fort Benning in military family housing. Our bedroom faces west. The thermostat is in the hall, and it can't be set below seventy-eight degrees for air-conditioning. But when it's seventy-eight in the hall, it's ninety-five in the bedroom."

"That's terrible!"

"Well, sir, it's actually not so bad. I bought a little table and lamp I put right under the thermostat, and I leave the lamp on all the time. Now when it's seventy-eight degrees at the thermostat, it's a cool sixty-nine in the bedroom."

For years, I had heard people from the military departments whining about "micromanagement," but shrugged it off as the inevitable complaints from the troops about the brass.

In fact, a previous boss, Bill Brehm, had been determined to reduce the size of OSD, and I had argued with him that the Pentagon needed more, not less, management. How wrong that turned out to be!

Yet even as I thought that more management was needed, I saw that it was worse than silly for people in Washington, D.C., to make decisions about whether people in Hawaii or Georgia were cool enough. So I shifted the efforts to decentralize decision authority into high gear.

My office had issued a rulebook called the *Construction Criteria Manual*—450 pages of how-tos and must-nots covering every imaginable aspect of buildings, from thermostat settings in residences to, as I was to learn, bowling alley design.

I told the admiral who headed the construction office to streamline the 450-page manual. He convened a working group from OSD and the military departments to review it and cut it down to the essentials. After a year, he presented me with the streamlined version—a not-so-slim 380 pages. I wasn't very happy, but I figured a seventy-page reduction was worth something, so I signed my approval and the new *Construction Criteria Manual* went into effect.

I should have known better. I soon learned.

I was in Comiso, Sicily, where the United States had built a brand new airbase for the cruise missiles that NATO was hurriedly deploying to counter the new Soviet intermediate-range missiles. I was being briefed about progress on the base construction and on changes to the original plan.

One of the changes was to tear out the wall of the sparkling new bowling center and double its size, from eight to sixteen lanes. I was appalled.

"You just built this bowling center. Why did you build it too small?" I asked Charlie Gibowitz, a super-competent naval officer and the Comiso construction engineer.

Charlie explained that it had been sized—as it was required to be—in accordance with the *Construction Criteria Manual*, which allowed one bowling lane for every 250 troops. Comiso was planned for a complement of 2,000 airmen, ergo eight bowling lanes.

Probably not a bad rule, on the average. The trouble was that Comiso—like every base—wasn't average. It was in the center of Sicily, miles from anything that would interest a nineteen-year-old airman. The base wasn't even very close to the little town of Comiso. And so the airmen, with their families back in the States and little to occupy their off-duty hours, took to bowling in a big way. And so a brand-new building was being torn up and expanded.

I made a mental note to do something about the manual when I had a chance. A couple of weeks later, I was back at the Pentagon holding my Monday staff meeting. Gerry Kauvar, one of the directors, was regaling us with his experience of Saturday night.

"Susan [his wife] and I were at the grand opening of the remodeled Fort Belvoir dining room and kitchen. The food was as bad as ever. After dinner, we were invited to see the new kitchen. It was beautiful. Only trouble was, it was ninety degrees outside and must have been 110 degrees in the kitchen. Stupid Army didn't air-condition the kitchen. No wonder the food was so bad."

This was too much for Robin Cababa, a fiery Army engineer officer who was my military assistant.

"IT'S YOUR RULE, SIR," he shouted. "They were following the rule in YOUR construction manual."

It was time for action. I told Doug Farbrother to fix it. Doug was even more fanatic than I was about clarity and brevity. Earlier he had come across DOD's policy on termite control, which ran to fifty-odd pages. Doug was certain it could be boiled down to two words: NO TERMITES. It put our whole environmental staff in a panic until they could persuade him that termiticides were far too toxic to humans to allow a two-word policy regarding their application.

But Doug's conviction and enthusiasm for simplification was unshaken. In a few days, he had cut the 380-page manual to eight pocket-size pages. He showed me a mockup of the book as he wanted it issued: pocket-size with a bright yellow cover.

All DOD publications had a "government" look about them. I had searched for a way to make the reports coming out of the installations organization distinctive, and my research confirmed that nobody in DOD ever bound a report in a yellow cover. Yellow stood for cowardice, and it was *never* used. So I chose yellow, and everybody who saw a yellow report knew it had come from the installations organization. Doug named the color "Installations Gold," but it was really yellow.

"This is all the guidance they need," Doug proudly announced. "And I've sized it to fit in the breast pocket of a BDU [battle dress uniform, the uniform worn by just about everybody on military bases, but never in the Pentagon] so base commanders can carry it everywhere."

I read it eagerly. It seemed to cover everything. It started with a vision for military bases:

> Military bases are hometowns.[1] They should have all the facilities a good town has—not just housing, but land and buildings designed for recreation, cultural and religious activities, education, health care, shopping, and work. Military bases ought to be the kind of towns you would want your sons and daughters to work and live in.

It defined excellence in terms of the customers' wishes, instead of the technicians' expertise:

> You cannot plan, design, or build an excellent facility unless you thoroughly understand what the customers want. Spend a lot of time finding out. Ask the unit commanders, the NCOs [noncommissioned officers], the young officers and enlisted people, and their families, how to make things better. The facility is excellent only if the customers say it is.

It handled the craziness I had run into over energy conservation:

> Design to cut energy use, while providing pleasant, comfortable living and working environments. And remember the first rule of energy conservation—don't hassle the troops. Give them plenty of light and let them adjust the temperature. If you have people working in the dark or if they're too cold or too hot, you are wasting a resource far more costly and valuable than energy.

It solved the Comiso bowling alley problem, too:

> The best guide to sizing is an existing facility that is satisfying the people who use it. Whatever the facility, find the best example you can and ask the people who use it how to make the next one better. If possible, use examples from America's best-run, profit-making companies. Remember to ask the customers—the commanders, the NCOs, the troops—what they want. Don't make buildings too small. An undersized building is more wasteful than an oversized one because people are more expensive than buildings.

Finally it reminded people in the Pentagon who was in charge:

> The commanding officer is responsible for accomplishing the mission of the installation and is accountable for all resources applied to the mission, and must have the authority to make investment decisions.

I loved it. The next step was to promulgate the little booklet as official DOD policy. The secretary of defense had signed a directive giving me authority to issue the construction manual after "coordinating" with and resolving differences between the various elements of OSD and the military departments.

So we circulated the manual and waited for the responses to come in. I had thought I was striking a blow against micromanagement and would have many allies in the military. But I learned that micromanagement was what somebody did to *you*. It was never something *you* did to others.

And so the Army and Navy construction people didn't like the eight-page version. It was all very well for me to devolve decision authority to the service headquarters, but not to require them to devolve it to the men and women in the field. The assistant secretaries of the Army and Navy responsible for military construction objected violently to the new guidance; so did the DOD comptroller and IG.

Only the Air Force and the DOD general counsel concurred with the little yellow book—the Air Force because its construction people were more sympathetic to the base commanders than those in the Army and Navy and because Chief-of-Staff Larry Welch was a true believer in putting authority and responsibility at the front line, which the manual did with a vengeance. The general counsel concurred because George Schlossberg, the only lawyer I knew in OSD who had any sense of helping the client or the troops, had helped me plan the whole thing.

Since I had the authority to resolve disagreements, I resolved them in favor of the manual, signed the official document making it official DOD policy, and sent it to the directives office to be issued.

Bad news. The woman who ran the directives office refused to issue it, saying she "just couldn't" issue a policy that the IG and comptroller both objected to. I showed her the directive from the secretary of defense giving me the authority, but she held her ground.

By now I had become enamored by the little yellow book. I had been counting on distributing it to an upcoming conference of installation commanders at El Toro Marine Corps Air Station in southern California. I knew the commanders would love it, because it put the commander in charge of his or her base. The mythology of command was that the commanders were in charge; the yellow book would strengthen their control.

As anxious as I was to get the manual out for the conference, I just didn't see a way around the directives woman. She didn't accept my clear authority to resolve disagreements, and there was no way the IG or comptroller would ever agree to its release.

I figured she controlled the printing press, but printing was just a matter of money. How expensive could it be? I could always pay the printing bill out of my own pocket.

I called in Tom Bee, who was managing the project, and handed him my check for $300.

"Talk to some commercial printers and find out how many of the books we could get for $300. But we must have them in time for the conference week after next."

Tom was shocked at the notion of privately printing official DOD documents, but he made some calls and reported that my $300 would pay for 1,900 little yellow books.

A few days later, Tom showed up with a box filled with the booklets. We all started to laugh uncontrollably at the incongruity. They sure didn't look like any DOD directives anybody had ever seen.

Tom handed me *his* check for $180, saying that the construction office wanted to pitch in and share the expense. I was touched to learn that the same team that had, only two years before, endorsed fixed thermostats and review of construction drawings by OSD now shared my commitment to revolutionary delegation of authority to base commanders.

Normally it takes a year or two for new DOD rules to trickle down to the front lines. Naturally, I didn't want to wait a year or two. Who does?

We held a mailing jamboree. I invited the construction team to my office where we set up an assembly line, stuffing, addressing, and sealing envelopes and carting them off to the mailroom. In a couple of hours, little yellow books were in the mail to every base commander and to every general and admiral I knew—more than 1,600 copies.

And just one more—I sent a copy to Will Taft, the deputy secretary of defense, who had totally embraced the general principle of power to the front lines. I wrote him that the manuals had been printed privately, that the first one was free, but that any more would cost him fifteen cents each. He sent the manual to his speechwriter with a note to work it into a future speech.

I was on top of the world. I carried extra copies of the now official little yellow book to my commanders' conference and handed them out to great hilarity and celebration. We were vanquishing the headquarters beast.

After the conference, I was on a victory lap of sorts. The commander of Camp Pendleton Marine Base was showing me around the huge military reservation in his jeep when his portable phone rang. It was for me.

"That little book of yours is causing quite an uproar. Come see me when you get back to the Pentagon. Meanwhile you'd better not distribute it."

Oops. It was my new boss, Bob Costello, late of General Motors. He seemed to be committed to making DOD more like GM, while I was committed to making it much, much less like GM. We were on a collision path.

"Well, Bob," I protested. "It's a little late for that. We've already distributed it."

"Well, don't distribute it any further!"

"OK, but you should understand, we've mailed out 1,600 copies—to every base commander around the world and to lots of others."

Costello was in a fury, and he had a right to be. I hadn't told him anything about what I was doing with the manual. I was absolutely certain (maybe I shouldn't have been, but I was) that he would see publishing the booklet as a very un-GM thing to do and side with the objectors, who included his principal colleagues, the assistant secretaries of the Army and Navy.

Therefore, I had tried to follow the advice of Admiral Grace Hopper, who had gained some fame with her watchword: It's easier to get forgiveness than permission.

Well, not always. I later repeated the phrase to another assistant secretary for whom I worked, and he bellowed at me, "NOT FROM ME IT ISN'T." So too with Costello. Permission would have been very unlikely, and forgiveness was impossible.

"You've got everybody in the Pentagon mad at you," he accused.

"No, the Air Force loves me and the Army and Navy combat officers," I unwisely snapped back. "Only the construction engineers are unhappy." That only made him madder.

"You're trashing the people you and I have to work with. You can't do business that way. Maybe you should rescind it."

"I can't do that."

He realized that if *he* rescinded the manual it would damage his reputation as a reformer. He ordered me to do what I had to in order to get the Army and Navy to agree to its publication.

I went back to my office and called my mentor and biggest supporter, General Bill Creech, the commander of Tactical Air Command (TAC). (How General Creech came to be my mentor is covered in chapter 4.) He advised me to compromise.

"Don't go down in flames with all guns blazing. We need you to fight another day."

But to me it felt impossible to compromise on the manual. I was convinced it was right, and I saw backing down as backing away from my principles— which I just couldn't do.

I called in Captain Mike Dallam, my new director of construction (having replaced the admiral), who had very good working relationships with the Army and Navy construction people.

I told Dallam he needed to get Army and Navy agreement, but to let them know I couldn't back down.

In *1984* George Orwell coined a number of phrases he called "Slogans of the Party." War is peace, freedom is slavery, and so on. My slogan became "weakness is strength." I had nothing to offer the Army and Navy, nothing to compromise about. The only thing I could give them was my job. If they held to their position, then I would probably be fired.

That was a little too much for them. The next guy probably would be worse. Dallam got them to agree to practically everything. We accepted a couple of changes that actually made it better. I forwarded their signed agreements to Costello. From his assistant came the final word: "OK, but NO LITTLE YELLOW BOOK. IT'S GOTTA BE ON 8-1/2-BY-11 PAPER."

I wanted—really wanted—a little yellow book, but I thought about Bill Creech's advice, and decided I could back down that much. It became a four-page manual replacing a 380-pager.

Our midnight mailing had been effective. For years, in places from Korea to Florida to Germany, people came up to me with the little yellow book, telling me how it had empowered them to do the right thing for their customers and their bases.

LESSONS FROM CHAPTER TWO:
SHRINKING REGULATIONS

—Ask the people who are regulated about the regulations; they'll have different opinions than people at headquarters.

—The best decisions are made by the people closest to the action with the biggest stake in the outcome.

—Headquarters rules often drive people in the field to do foolish things.

—Regulations that tie workers hands have a determined constituency. It takes the top person with a wild look in the eye to eliminate them.

NOTE

1. This un-DOD-like idea of bases being hometowns came from Army colonel Tom Fincher, base commander at Fort Leavenworth, Kansas, who was as fanatic as anyone on the subject of excellence.

3

Red Hats, Red Scarves, Red Tails

(Organizing for the Mission)

"Have you lost your mind? Red hats, red scarves, red tails? That's the dumbest thing I ever heard. What did those Air Force guys do to you?"

Doug Farbrother was angry. I had been pursuing his and my plan for improving management when I had been—to put it plainly—hijacked. And here I was, sympathizing with the hijackers.

Doug and I, like almost everybody in OSD, had bought into the accepted management theories of the day. They had their basis in arguably the most successful American corporation of the twentieth century, General Motors (GM). GM's management style was taught in all the best business schools and admired in all the business press. GM's stock was the very definition of "blue chip."

The principles were few and obvious: since management was good, more management must be better; since analysis was good, more analysis must be better; duplication was bad; specialization was good; small organizations should be combined into big organizations with great economies of scale. And if you got the inputs (capital and labor) in the right amounts and in the right places, and if you told the workers exactly how to do the job, the outputs would take care of themselves.

To go with our management theories, we had the traditional mistrust that headquarters had for the field. Commanders especially were not to be trusted.

The first actions of the incoming Reagan administration had been to increase defense spending by $30 billion, big money in those days. Military readiness was dangerously low—troops were underpaid and poorly housed, and many planes, tanks, and ships were sidelined due to lack of parts. The new money was to go to restore readiness.

By 1982, it seemed reasonable to ask where the money had gone, so Deputy Secretary of Defense Frank Carlucci asked the IG to find out.

The IG confirmed our worst fears—commanders were frittering away the readiness money on such frills as refinishing gym floors and replating salute cannons. There even was a crazy general at Langley Air Force Base in Virginia who was squandering the readiness money on huge quantities of paint, some of which he was applying to the backs of stop signs.

In the defense system, operational commanders—such as division or wing commanders—were also in charge of base operations: building maintenance, feeding, housing, medical care, roads and runways, and laundry facilities; the list was a mile long. It appeared to me that none of the commanders in the field seemed the least bit cost conscious. The commanders and their equally guilty advocates at headquarters would fight like hell for the biggest budget they could possibly justify, then the commanders would work like hell to make sure they spent every nickel. The system seemed to guarantee waste.

For months I searched in vain for a commander who defied my model—one who was cost conscious.

I wound up one day at the U.S. naval communication activity in Edzell, Scotland, a little base where a few hundred sailors, fluent in Russian, monitored electronic transmissions from the Soviet military. The base sparkled with energy and efficiency. The officers were sensible and knew their troops, their mission, and their management challenges. Surely here I would find the cost consciousness I was looking for.

"I'm looking for a commander who makes saving money a priority, somebody who will find ways he can spend less and keep things almost as good," I explained to the commander.

He thought for a minute, because he didn't want to disappoint this visitor from Washington who could cause unknown trouble for him. But he answered honestly, as commanders always did.

"You've come to the wrooooonnng place," he drawled.

Traveling to the field can be enlightening, and I recommend it to anyone with a leadership or management responsibility. You can't find out what's really going on from reports. You've got to see for yourself in order to understand.

Unfortunately, people's minds work in odd ways: often they fit new information to old prejudices. That's what I did with the Edzell experience. Rather than conclude that I had been looking for the wrong thing, I decided that even outstanding commanders, as the Edzell commander surely was, had the wrong set of incentives.

Perhaps the cure was more centralization: take the bases away from operational commanders and create a defense agency to run them. There were already defense agencies for logistics, intelligence, audit, and several other functions that involved more than one of the military departments. By and large, the agencies didn't deal with the individual service member. That had traditionally been left to the individual services—Army, Navy, Air Force, and Marine Corps.

The services didn't like defense agencies because the agencies controlled functions that the services would have preferred to keep. They really hated the idea of a base-operating agency, arguing that it would erode their abilities to take care of the troops. The Air Force believed that only Air Force people could be deeply committed to care for Air Force members. The other services held similar beliefs, although not as strongly as the Air Force, which was fanatically dedicated to the welfare of its people.

I countered with the argument that's always made to justify centralization. First, the agency would be run by professionals in base operations, much like professional city managers. Leaders of infantry, aviation, submarines, and the like would be freed for their duties as war fighters. And second, there would be huge savings from economies of scale as we ended duplication. No longer would every base have its own personnel office, laundry, housing office, procurement office, and so on. Bigger was better (remember GM!), and the base-operating agency would be the biggest of all.

I had another theory for handling particularly tough assignments from my days as a heat transfer engineer. The theory was that if you assign a problem to somebody who is very smart and who has a stake in the outcome, and that person can't solve it, then the assignment was impossible.

The assignment: make the best case possible for forming a base-operations agency under OSD, then stand back and decide whether the case was convincing.

I turned to Irv Greenberg, my old mentor, who had taught me most of what I knew about getting things done in the Pentagon and then groomed me to succeed him as deputy assistant secretary of defense.

Irv had retired and was working as a consultant to DOD and was eager to help. I also assigned Doug to the job. Doug was a fanatic about putting all the bases under a defense agency—in fact he wanted to head the agency.

We needed some cover for the effort, because we knew the military departments would scream bloody murder about what we were doing. That was easy for skilled bureaucrats. We went to Paul Thayer, the deputy secretary of defense, and explained how inefficient the military was at running bases, how a single central agency *might* be more efficient, and how the military departments would likely tell him we were doing something that would bring the nation's defense to its knees.

In the trade, this process of prewarning is called "inoculation." We warned the boss that people would tell him we were crazy. Then when people actually told him we were crazy, it only confirmed to him how wise we were.

It worked. Thayer gave us the go ahead, and when the military complained, he brushed off their complaints.

We went to work.

Irv, who had served with General Douglas MacArthur in World War II, was an analyst with a deep respect for history. He searched the archives and learned that the Army had operated during the war with a base-operating agency called the Army Service Command. It made sense then, Irv explained, because the Army was forming new force units (divisions) on the bases, then shipping the divisions off to war. Even then, the Army had trouble with its own Army Air Corps (the forerunner of the Air Force), which wanted its own wing commanders to run its bases. The arguments continued throughout the war, with correspondence even reaching George Marshall, the wartime chief of staff. This experience forecast well the vehemence of the Air Force opposition to our proposal forty years later.

Irv also was a whiz with numbers and data. He pored over data that OSD maintained on DOD activities that had been reviewed for possible contracting out. Nobody had ever paid any attention to the data before, and it was a mess. But Irv got it in his teeth like a terrier and wouldn't let go. After weeks of stewing, massaging, retabulating, and generally analyzing, Irv had the "smoking gun"!

He discovered that DOD activities that were reviewed for contracting out became twenty-seven percent cheaper on average, whether they ultimately were contracted out or whether they remained in house. We called this solid evidence of inefficiency "the efficiency gap" and ran to Thayer with the data to strengthen our case for some kind of change.

Meanwhile, Doug was busy traveling. He had learned that neither of our two biggest military allies, the United Kingdom and Germany, allowed local commanders to run their bases; both had centralized control under independent agencies. He went to see for himself.

In the United Kingdom, military bases were run by the Property Services Administration (PSA), the British version of America's General Services Administration. The British military that Doug met all hated the PSA with a passion. It was remote, inefficient, and unresponsive to the needs of local commanders—not a very promising model for us.

The German centralization model was more interesting. In line with the German passion for acronyms, it was called STOV, short for Standortverwaltung. It was a civilian organization under the Ministry of Defense (MOD). Surely it would be better accepted than the U.K. version. STOV members briefed Doug on how efficient they were and how well accepted by the German military. Doug was quite impressed, although his confidence was shaken a bit near the end of his trip when a German Air Force colonel, who had spent some time assigned to Air Force bases in the United States, took him aside out of earshot of the official MOD escort and whispered, "Please, please, don't do this to my American friends."

Doug came home impressed with STOV, but a little concerned that the German colonel had been so passionate an opponent of the German approach.

However, we didn't have to rely completely on evidence from allies. There was a small American model to study.

San Antonio had five major military bases: four Air Force (Brooks, Kelly, Randolph, and Lackland), and Fort Sam Houston, a large Army training base. Each base operated independently of the others with its own personnel office, procurement office, housing management office, building maintenance, base laundry, and so on. This so-called duplication had aroused a lot of criticism from Congress and the GAO. Several years earlier, the Air Force had yielded a little to the pressure for centralization by combining all building maintenance for the five bases under a new San Antonio Real Property Management Agency, or SARPMA.

SARPMA was mildly disliked by the Army people whom it supported and intensely despised by the Air Force (in spite of its being an Air Force operation). But it was a model to examine, so following Pentagon protocol, I informed Air Force headquarters that I would like to visit SARPMA.

The Air Force offered to fly me to San Antonio in a snazzy executive jet. On the way, our jet made an unscheduled diversion to Langley Air Force Base. I was told we needed to make a short stop for some minor maintenance.

But when we landed at Langley, there seemed to be no hurry to move on. Colonel Bud Ahearn, my Air Force escort, suggested we might as well, as long as we were there, pay a call on Lieutenant General John Piotrowski, the vice commander of TAC, headquartered at Langley.

It didn't occur to me to be surprised that we could just drop in without notice on the vice commander of the Air Force's biggest command or to be surprised that our plane needed a bit of maintenance in the middle of a flight from Washington, D.C., to San Antonio. It was no surprise at all to the Air Force, where it had all been carefully planned.

General Piotrowski greeted me warmly and proceeded to show me a briefing that would destroy all my attitudes toward management.

TAC was turning conventional wisdom (and mine) on its head. First, General Bill Creech, the TAC commander, was the "crazy general" the DOD IG had discovered spending the Reagan budget increase on paint. Creech spruced up TAC's whole physical plant to help generate pride, because, he preached, "Pride is the fuel of human accomplishment."

Creech had taken over a command that was suffering—like the rest of the U.S. military—from a "highly centralized management system, structure, and style that was strangling motivation, leadership, and creativity, and thereby wreaking havoc on quality and productivity."[1]

He implemented a decentralized, leadership approach in all TAC activities, from planning training flights to stocking spare parts.

He reorganized the entire command to give everyone a sense of ownership and association with TAC's flying mission. TAC, no less than OSD, had fallen victim to the McNamara-era fad for centralization and homogenization in the false name of efficiency. Each wing told itself it was a great performer, but had no answer when Creech asked, "Compared to what?"

Most of the people in the wing had been part of a huge centralized maintenance organization that was responsible for all the wing's eighty-odd aircraft. It operated like old Mr. Hobson, who offered customers at his stable the choice of the horse next to the door or none at all.

Creech decentralized maintenance into three identical aircraft maintenance units, or AMUs, called Red, Blue, or Gold according to the colored ball
caps the airmen wore. Then he divvied up the airplanes and painted their tails
red, blue, or gold. Finally he assigned the pilots to three groups and identified
them by the red, blue, or gold scarves they wore.

Each wing had three teams, identical except for their colors. The new teams
"owned" their planes and felt responsible and accountable for them. There
was now an answer to Creech's "compared to what?" The teams could be compared to each other. In front of every AMU's hangar sprouted a scoreboard in
the team's color showing the current month's performance. Anyone driving
down the line of hangars could instantly see which unit was in first, second,
or third place that month. Soon there was a scoreboard in front of the base
commissary where everybody in the wing, every family member, and every
visitor could see the score. Competition produced what it's supposed to: drastically increased performance.

All TAC's performance measures started to rise and would continue to rise.
Percent of aircraft that were mission capable, flights per month per aircraft,
percent of broken aircraft fixed within eight hours, as well as other measures,
were all up by forty percent or more.

At the time of my visit, August 1982, the effect of the Reagan budget increases had yet to be felt, except for the paint. Massive quantities of spare parts
would not arrive in Air Force parts bins for another year. So TAC made these
dramatic improvements with no more people, little more money, and an actual *decline* in the experience level of airmen in the command.

Though the only inputs that increased were paint and pride, the outputs
were going through the roof. (By 1984, two years after my visit and six years
after Creech took command, TAC's combat capability had doubled, due
mainly to Creech's organizational changes and leadership.[2])

Creech described what he did as organizing around the human spirit, in
contrast to the methods of Frederick Taylor and GM, which treated the human spirit as irrelevant at best, and a nuisance at worst.[3]

General Piotrowski described the TAC rebirth in down-to-earth terms: "We
have pilots with red scarves flying airplanes with red tails maintained by mechanics with red caps."

By the end of my hour with General Piotrowski, I was grateful that my airplane (which was not one of TAC's) had developed a sudden need for repairs,

and grateful to Piotrowski for opening my eyes to what I later came to understand and describe as the greatest U.S. military success story since the Inchon landing in Korea in 1950.

I said goodbye to the general and, the plane magically restored to operability, flew off to San Antonio to see DOD's best effort at centralization, SARPMA.

If ever a centralized base agency could work, it was SARPMA. The Air Force had given it every chance to work. It was commanded by an outstanding, customer-oriented engineer officer. The chain of command was short—the SARPMA commander reported directly to the four-star commander of the Air Training Command. SARPMA and all its customers were located close together, right in San Antonio.

There would be—everybody thought—economies of scale. SARPMA could afford to write off the purchase of modern labor-saving equipment over five bases instead of the usual one. And the bigger customer base meant that work could be scheduled more efficiently and with less down time.

At SARPMA, we heard briefings that seemed to show small, but real increases in efficiency. Fortunately, I had the presence of mind to ask what the customers—the commanders of the five bases—thought.

"Ah, you know, you just can't satisfy the commanders, no matter how good a job you do. We serve them at least as well as their own organizations did in the old days before SARPMA, but they don't appreciate it because we're not part of their organization."

Seemed reasonable enough, but I was unprepared for the venom the customers spewed out about SARPMA. Typical was the story that Major General Carl Smith, the Lackland Air Force Base commander, told.

When his predecessor moved out and the Lackland commander's house was being readied for General Smith, SARPMA noticed that the carpet in the living room was badly worn in the center (where most carpets wear out first) from the many official gatherings that the general held. So, they cut out a big circle of worn material and stitched in a new piece that was a slightly different color.

General Smith was unhappy with the big circle of mismatched carpet in the middle of his living room and informed SARPMA that the whole carpet needed replacement. SARPMA offered to replace the carpet at General Smith's expense and, of course, report the unnecessary replacement to Congress, which watched closely what was spent to maintain generals' housing.

I concluded that if SARPMA wouldn't (or couldn't) satisfy a major general, what chance for satisfaction did a captain or a sergeant have? And if an organization couldn't satisfy its customers, it sure wasn't something I wanted to emulate.

I returned to the Pentagon, hijacked but happily educated in the wonders of a new style of organization and leadership based on decentralization, deregulation, and delegation of authority within an atmosphere of strong and clear values. I now understood the failings of the old centralization model I had been pushing hard. Since I now knew that a base-operating agency was a bad idea, there was no need to continue with our study, which was earning us enmity all through the military departments.

I couldn't wait to tell Doug what I had learned, certain that he would see things the same way as I did—just like always. I had a very simple summary, but Doug exploded at my report.

"Have you lost your mind? Red hats, red scarves, red tails? That's the dumbest thing I ever heard. What did those Air Force guys do to you?"

I was shaken. I wasn't used to Doug disagreeing with me. I usually fed on his agreement to renew energy and confidence to tackle the huge job I had.

I could feel the conviction I had returned with dissolving into mere inclination. The new ideas that had seemed so clear at Langley and San Antonio turned hazy in the Pentagon. I decided to continue with the study.

The Air Force hijacking had failed! More direct measures were called for. From Langley came a summons: General Bill Creech, Commander of TAC, would like Doug to visit to discuss the agency study.

Doug returned from Langley a different person. Where I had returned with a new idea, Doug came back with a new religion. We had both listened for months to military complaints about the idea of an agency and pleas to put local commanders in absolute charge of their bases, and they hadn't made a dent in our skulls. But an hour for me with Piotrowski and a day for Doug with Creech was enough to turn us around for good.

Doug wrote, "It didn't take him [Creech] long to shake the very foundations of my OSD management articles of faith. After hearing him talk, and seeing the evidence for myself, I lost interest in the 'economies of scale' and all zeal for centralized management."

So did I.

So we abandoned the study.

Bill Creech would later tell me, "There's a war on between the people who are trying to do something and the people who are trying to keep them from doing anything wrong." Just a few weeks later I was to discover a new book that would build on Creech's influence and land me squarely in the middle of that war, on the side of the people in the field and opposing most of the people in OSD.

LESSONS FROM CHAPTER THREE: ORGANIZING FOR THE MISSION

—Pride is the fuel of human accomplishment.[4]

—The best organizations support the human spirit, not oppose it.

—You can't learn what's going on at the front line from reports; you have to see for yourself. Commanders and local managers will always tell you what's *really* going on.

—Centralizing support services always makes them less responsive to local commanders/managers, and therefore less effective. Economies of scale are always promised, but rarely materialize.

—Measuring results makes them improve, and comparing results makes them take off.[5] If you have centralized, consolidated, one-of-a-kind organizations, you have no like organizations to compare them to.

NOTES

1. Bill Creech, *The Five Pillars of TQM: How to Make Total Quality Management Work for You* (New York: Truman Talley Books/Dutton, 1994), 116.

2. David Osborne and Ted Gaebler, *Reinventing Government: How the Entrepreneurial Spirit is Transforming the Public Sector* (Reading, Mass.: Addison Wesley, 1992), 257–259.

3. Creech's experience has been described by Tom Peters and Nancy Austin in *A Passion for Excellence: The Leadership Difference* (New York: Random House, 1985).

4. I owe this to General Bill Creech.

5. This too.

4

Searching for Excellence

(Turning an Organization Around)

The private sector has it all over government when it comes to management. That's because the market imposes change on the private sector: if companies don't change, they die. The nation as a whole benefits from what economist Joseph Schumpeter has called "creative destruction."

Government, on the other hand, is largely immune to market forces and, therefore, to creative destruction. That's not all bad. If a government agency—DOD, for example—is inefficient, we don't want it subjected to creative destruction, we want it fixed. Like many others, I believed that studying the best private-sector practices could help me fix my own department.

That's why I rushed to buy a copy of *In Search of Excellence: Lessons from America's Best-Run Companies* by Tom Peters and Bob Waterman (Harper & Row, 1982), as soon as I saw it reviewed in *The Economist* in 1983.[1] The book was a quick read, a fascinating compilation of stories that the authors billed as "secrets of America's best-run companies."

I knew it was important the moment I finished it, but I couldn't figure out exactly what to do with it. I turned for advice to Gerry Kauvar, one of the eight directors in the installations organization, a voracious reader, and a big thinker. Gerry suggested I get all eight directors to read it—then maybe we could figure it out together at an offsite.

One small problem: the books cost $19.95 each, and it would take a long time—maybe forever—to get the government to buy them for us. I was in a hurry; I believed that anything worth doing is worth doing fast. So I sprang for the $159.60 plus $6.39 tax for eight copies of *In Search of Excellence* and gave them to the directors, asking them to read the book in preparation for an offsite in two weeks.

Peters and Waterman were with McKinsey and Company, so one of the installations directors, Pete Daley, called his old college buddy, Jay Abbe, now with McKinsey, for help. Abbe, along with his McKinsey coworker, Ron Bancroft, volunteered to come to the Pentagon and coach us on how to use *In Search of Excellence*.

The book was subtitled *Lessons from America's Best-Run Companies*, and it was organized, after some introductory material, into eight chapters, one for each of the eight traits it identified as hallmarks of excellent companies. The traits are: "a bias for action"; "close to the customer"; "autonomy and entrepreneurship"; "productivity through people"; "hands-on value driven"; "stick to the knitting"; "simple form and lean staff"; and "simultaneous loose-tight properties."

After a short discussion, Bancroft and Abbe administered a simple test to the team: we were to grade ourselves on a scale of one to ten on each of the eight traits. We scored lowest on "close to the customer" and "hands-on value driven," so they suggested we spend the offsite working on those two traits: a half-day to identify our customers, and a half-day to figure out what our values were.

At the offsite, the customer discussion turned into a wrangle over whether we even had customers—a radical idea at the time—and who they might be. Half the team thought we didn't have customers, and if we did, then they were Congress, the secretary of defense, or the American people. The other half thought our customers should be the troops. I resolved it: our customers from now on would be "the soldiers, sailors, marines, and airmen who defend America."

The discussion about values was all over the place. Coming into the meeting, some thought we should work for efficiency, some thought quality, some thought saving money, and some thought spending more to take care of the troops. The defense culture was to provide a minimum acceptable level of comfort and quality: the roofs shouldn't leak; on the other hand, troops could be packed two or three adults to a small room. DOD's traditional approach to creature comfort was to figure out what discomfort level would be just bad enough to make troops leave the military in droves, then provide just a tiny bit more comfort so that the bad things didn't happen. DOD and the Office of

Management and Budget (OMB) had been applying the same logic to military pay and benefits for years, with disastrous results.

The dreadful state of the military had been a major issue in the 1980 election, and the new Reagan administration had rushed through the biggest military pay raise in years, along with billions of dollars to increase readiness. But the "minimum essential" culture still ruled the Pentagon, especially in the offices of the comptroller and IG.

It had ruled me as well. Until I had been strong-armed into taking the installations job I had been a believer in "minimum essential," analyzing proposed pay raises to make sure there wasn't a dollar more than was needed to keep the troops from bailing out, and in general, making sure that there was nothing in the budget that wasn't absolutely "necessary."

One of my first issues as deputy assistant secretary of defense for Installations was to set standards for UPHs. UPH was DOD slang for what the Army, Navy, and Marine Corps called barracks and the Air Force called dormitories. The Air Force thought "barracks" connoted a lack of dignity for the people living there; the Army, Navy, and Marine Corps thought "dormitories" connoted sissiness. So OSD came up with the neutral term "unaccompanied personnel housing," which became, of course, UPHs.

UPHs were a major budget issue, housing as they did about 500,000 troops. I signed a new standard that provided more space and privacy than the current standards of the time, but not nearly as much as the Air Force wanted. I thought that would be good enough.

My visits to TAC had shaken my beliefs in centralization. Next, General Bill Creech and his chief engineer, Major General Jud Ellis, had started to unravel my faith in economic analysis and my commitment to minimum essential with TAC's obvious commitment to what looked to me like excess: excess paint, excess service to the troops, and excess commitment to the troops' standard of living.

But *In Search of Excellence* pushed me over the top with its exposition of how excellent companies displayed "a seemingly unjustifiable over-commitment to some form of quality, reliability, or service."[2] One example that made a lasting impression on me was the story of Frito-Lay's service "overkill":

> Frito will do some things that in the short run are uneconomic. It will spend
> several hundred dollars sending a truck to restock a store with a couple of

thirty-dollar cartons of potato chips. There are magic and symbolism about the service call that cannot be quantified. As we said earlier, it is a cost analyst's dream target. You can always make a case for saving money by cutting back a percentage point or two. But Frito management, looking at market shares and margins, won't tamper with the zeal of the sales force.[3]

There it was! *I* had been the cost analyst cutting back on zeal. But no longer. The book and our conversations about it had finally crystallized the issue for me and had resolved in my mind the conflict between quality and waste. I knew now there was no conflict.

The eight installations directors and I wrestled with the issue of values for the rest of the day, but we couldn't resolve it. I told them I wanted to concentrate on three things: innovation, competition, and recognition. In the spirit of inclusiveness, I decided to settle the values question with a contest, open to all eighty people in the installations organization. I would put up $100 for the best statement of our values. Entries would close in two days.

The $100 prize energized the directors, and one of them, Duncan Holaday, proposed we end the offsite with a toast. He had come prepared for the occasion with a liqueur that had been used for toasting by General Frederick Kroesen, U.S. Army commander in Germany. The liqueur, called Ratzeputz, was 116 proof and caused steam to come out of one's ears. I wasn't sure what was the greatest accomplishment of the day, identifying our customer, arguing about our values, or swallowing a half ounce of Ratzeputz. The closing Ratzeputz toast became an Installations tradition, just like the yellow report covers. Ratzeputz is hard to find in the United States, but fortunately, Duncan's bottle went a long way.

The next day Pete Daley came to see me with a remarkable set of ideas that became our agenda for the next few years. First he showed me a proclamation, to be signed by the president (Pete always had big ideas), of an annual competition for the best base in each military service. The winners would get a new award—the Commander in Chief's Award for Installation Excellence.

I read over the proclamation. It was very good, but I thought I could make it a little better. Pete stood his ground. "Hey, put your pen down. I was up half the night polishing this. It fits together perfectly. Any change you make will make it worse, not better." So I put my pen down.

Pete called his second item "DOD Directive Number One." The idea was to deregulate base operations: we would have just one page of rules for base commanders to follow, instead of tens of thousands. It was a noble idea, but a little ahead of its time, as it turned out.

His third idea was the best. *In Search of Excellence* told how the McCrory's Company established one of its stores as a model store, where the manager and staff were given lots of freedom and were encouraged to visit the competition, learn, give their best, and use their heads.[4]

Pete proposed that we establish a model installation—a military base where innovation, one of our three goals, would be encouraged. I liked the idea. I had several ideas of my own I wanted to try—for example, giving military families in government housing a heating and electricity allowance, then charging them for what they consumed, instead of the current system of providing free utilities and hassling them to conserve.

That would be a win-win situation—the families would have a financial incentive to save energy. They could pocket the difference between the allowance and what they consumed, and the government would save because the allowances would be set below what the government had been spending. Free-market incentives would leave both the families and the government better off. It seemed like good old American free enterprise substituting for traditional military paternalism. Couldn't miss.

I had other ideas about replacing command-and-control paternalism with incentives and choice in military housing operations—a $5–10 billion a year operation. If these ideas worked as well as I thought they would, the troops would be happier and the government would save a bundle of money.

So I agreed that we should establish a model installation. There was only one thing in our way: I didn't control any installation. The military commands did, and they didn't trust OSD one bit. I would have to go out and sell the idea to some four-star generals.

Meanwhile, in just two days the contest to choose the best statement of our values had attracted more than a hundred entries from people in installations as well as in the military departments. Many people submitted more than one entry. Clearly I had touched a nerve, through the combination of the subject and the money. I had reserved for myself the choice of the winning entry and had little trouble narrowing the field to two: "Excellent Facilities," and "Installations: The Foundation of Defense."

I ruled that it was a tie. Each of the winning entrants would get $50, and I combined the key elements of both entries. Our value statement would be: "Excellent Installations: The Foundation of Defense."

It was a winner. The winners were happy, even though they had to share the $100, and there was a great deal of enthusiasm about our statement of values. DOD prizes symbols and paraphernalia. Within weeks we had an Excellent Installations seal—the DOD seal with "Excellent Installations: The Foundation of Defense" inscribed around it—which appeared on our stationery and on new lapel pins, pendants, cuff links, and, best of all, on baseball caps that everyone in installations wore everywhere, including all over the Pentagon. I even had coins made up bearing the new seal, which I could present to people who were advancing the cause.

People who saw us wearing the caps in the halls and offices of the Pentagon thought we were crazy, and I guess we were, a little. Several months later, I had the opportunity to brief the Defense Council on Integrity and Management Improvement (DCIMI) on the Model Installation Program (MIP). The DCIMI (pronounced dee-SIMMY), chaired by William Howard Taft IV, deputy secretary of defense, was as sober as its name. Its meetings usually included a series of mind-numbing briefings. I wanted the audience to be wide awake for my briefing and to remember it. They never forgot the guy in the baseball cap. That was a first for the Pentagon.

Now, knowing what my organization stood for and wearing my Excellent Installations baseball cap, I set off to find a general or admiral who would establish a model installation with me.

I worked on a briefing that would lay out what I was trying to do. It was a simple story. I was trying to create "Excellent Installations: The Foundation of Defense" using three factors: innovation (model installations), competition (mainly through comparisons of performance between bases), and recognition (the Commander in Chief's Award for Installations Excellence). Strikingly—for OSD—absent was any mention of rules, budgets, or reports.

I wanted to "test market" my briefing around the Pentagon. I had heard that Air Force Lieutenant General Larry Welch was the Air Force's thought leader, so I went first to see him. Welch loved the briefing, and offered several suggestions to improve it. (Welch would soon get his fourth star and appointment as Air Force vice chief of staff, then move to head the Strategic Air Command before becoming Air Force chief in 1986. His advice was always so good that I soon came to count on him for counsel whenever I was faced with a big problem or opportunity. He always made time for me and always came through with advice or encouragement, whichever I needed more.)

I then gave private briefings to about twenty senior leaders around the Pentagon, making modifications after each one. Finally, I was ready to take it on the road.

The military services were organized into major commands: TAC, the Army Forces Command, the Navy Training Command, and so forth. The heads of the commands normally controlled the bases on which their commands operated. So off I went to see them.

Most of the military leaders were cautious. Yes, my story sounded good and there didn't *seem* to be any risk for them, but still, I *was* from OSD, so how could they trust me? Especially since I was the one behind the infamous Carlucci memo (it might as well have been called the Stone memo) ordering a study of a defense agency that would grab all their bases. The word started to circulate among the cynics that I intended to start MIP to find the one best way to operate a base, then mandate that all bases be run exactly the same way—a neo-Taylorist plot.[5]

Whenever I briefed an Air Force general I got the same reaction: have you shown this to General Creech, and what does he think? Creech was the key: If he liked it, the Air Force would play. If the Air Force played, the Army would too, followed by the Marine Corps, and eventually the Navy. So I made an appointment to brief Creech.

Creech loved the idea. Setting up small test, or pilot, programs in a hurry was right up his alley. He had used the technique in TAC to gradually introduce massive change. He encouraged me to start with a few bases, then expand as the program established a record of success.

Then he asked a question that I should have been prepared for but wasn't. "What do you want me to do?"

I improvised. "Let's get together in three weeks. I'll bring you a prospectus defining the program, and you tell me what base you want to designate." We shook on the deal, and I went to work.

We needed a "tiger team." That's what the Pentagon called groups that were assembled ad hoc to work intensively for a short time to solve a pressing and important problem. I went over the roster of my organization and found the right leader: Air Force Colonel Ron Susi, a pilot, an excellent analyst, and a person who would have credibility with senior military officers. Then I called in the twelve most capable people in the organization and gave them their orders.

"Drop everything you're doing by the end of today. Tomorrow you'll go to work at 400 Army-Navy Drive [an office building where there was some unused space] to design a model installation: what it is, how it works, and how to get it started. Your job is to produce a prospectus that I can deliver to General Creech three weeks from today."

They dove into the assignment and delivered a six-page report on time. I delivered the report to General Creech on the appointed day, along with my digest of the report: a model installations "rulebook," which I had printed on a wallet-size card.

MODEL INSTALLATIONS: WHO DOES WHAT

Model Installations will
  • strive for excellence
  • try new methods, risk failures
  • use any savings to improve the installation
  • put up with visitors.

Headquarters will
  • help model commander get the authority he needs, quickly
  • not try to run the base or second guess the commander
  • protect planned budget, without pouring money in or skimming savings away
  • find out and publicize what's happening.

General Creech and I had agreed that the first model installation should be far from Washington, and he nominated Moody Air Force Base in Valdosta, Georgia.

We were on our way. Eleven days later—lightning speed for OSD—Deputy Secretary of Defense Paul Thayer signed a half-page memo to the military departments "offering each Service the opportunity to designate a few bases as 'model installations,'" and promising to "waive, as needed, regulations within my authority when good rationale is presented . . ." It was a radical departure from typical practice. "Offering" and "waive" were not traditional words in Pentagon directives.

Neither was our rulebook. The wallet-size card contained the only rules the program ever had—and all it ever needed.

We were soon proven right to have started with Creech. There was a demand from the other major Air Force commands to participate, and the Army, Marines, and Navy wanted in, too. Soon we had fifteen model installations, five Air Force, five Army, three Navy, and two Marine (i.e., five in each military department).

With Ron Susi's urging, I put everybody I could find to work on model installations. We visited each one, presented a special model installation flag that some Army friends stationed in Korea had purchased at cut rate, and helped them get started.

It turned out that nobody was interested in trying any of my ideas, but they sure had ideas of their own they wanted to try. We were quickly deluged with requests for waivers to apparently senseless rules.

The safety czars at the Pentagon had required Army recruits to take a military driving test and get a military driver's license, regardless of whether they had gotten state licenses as soon as they were eligible. Jack Mahoney had been a young transportation officer at Fort Sill, Oklahoma, in 1964 when he first proposed ending the practice. He kept trying but was turned down repeatedly until Fort Sill became a model installation in 1983, when he brought it up again. We approved his model installation proposal quickly and used the story to get top-level support for the program.

My favorite crazy rule required painters on the tank repair line at the Anniston, Alabama, Army Depot to get written approval from the base chemist before using a can of spray paint that was past its shelf "pull date." The chemist applied a computer-generated label that stated that the can had been "revalidated." This rule broadcast to all who heard it that they were expected to check their brains at the door when they came to work.

More than just crazy rules, the Pentagon system seemed designed to ensure that people in the field who knew what needed to be done couldn't act until they had gotten permission from people in Washington, D.C., who didn't have a clue. Jim Eddings, the base civil engineer at Kirtland Air Force Base in Albuquerque, New Mexico, saw some leaky roofs and wanted to have them repaired before they deteriorated or caused damage to materiel stored inside.

But he had to get approval from the deputy assistant secretary of the Air Force, who had no way of knowing whether the roofs needed repair except from what Eddings told him.

In the first two years, more than 8,000 model installation proposals were submitted to the Pentagon or to a major command; countless thousands more were approved by the base commander acting within existing authority. An unknowable number of times, people just used their heads, freed from the shackles of over-regulation and micromanagement.

These shackles had been crushing to the spirits and the output of three million people who lived and worked on military bases. When we freed people at the model installations from these burdens, we unleashed their creativity and enthusiasm and increased defense capability.

Tom Peters captured the spirit of MIP in his television show *Excellence in the Public Sector*.[6] He visited the naval air station at Alameda, California, a model installation, and interviewed Willie Carter. Carter's official title was P-3 aircraft maintenance division head, but he told Peters, "I'm the CEO of my business. I'm the guy calling the shots to see that my business makes money. If my business doesn't make money, I'm going to be looking at the shareholders."

In 1986, David Packard, chairman of the President's Blue Ribbon Commission on Defense Management, wrote in his final report to the president,

> Despite formidable bureaucratic obstacles, I believe that a 'centers of excellence approach' can tangibly improve productivity and quality. If widely adopted and steadfastly supported, it could achieve revolutionary progress throughout defense management. The potential applications are almost without number.
>
> In 1984, for example, DOD began to apply this concept to managing its installations as potential centers of excellence, by according installations commanders much greater latitude to run things their own way, cut through red tape, and experiment with new ways of accomplishing their mission. As a result, commanders and their personnel have found more effective means to do their jobs, identified wasteful regulations, and reduced costs while improving quality. The program has shown the increased defense capability that comes by freeing talented people from overregulation and unlocking their native creativity and enthusiasm.[7]

Packard was surely right about the potential applications being without number. The lessons of decentralization of authority and local initiative seem to apply everywhere. Whenever I describe MIP and what I learned from it, I connect with my audience. It may be General Joe Palastra, former commander in chief of Army forces in the United States, explaining that "It's Leadership 101 but nobody practices it," or Elysse Beasley explaining how the Pentagon works just like Smyrna High School in Tennessee where she teaches. It might be government workers in Eugene, Oregon, complaining that the people in Salem don't have a clue, or workers at the Miami International Airport complaining that the people downtown at the Miami–Dade Aviation Department don't understand what it's like at the airport.

Together with the establishment of a Commander in Chief's Award for Installation Excellence, we now had accomplished two of the three things that Pete Daley had proposed the day after our offsite in order to implement *In Search of Excellence*. Only DOD Directive Number One remained.

I loved the idea of a one-page directive, having borrowed the idea from *In Search of Excellence* and the story of Rene McPherson of Dana Corporation, who had thrown out twenty-two inches of policy manuals when he took over as CEO, and replaced them with a one-page philosophy statement. However, I wasn't satisfied with Pete's draft, and I didn't know how to fix it, so I had pigeonholed it. Whenever somebody from the military suggested that I had a hidden agenda, I would tell them, "My hidden agenda is to toss out 10,000 pages of regulations and substitute a one-page DOD Directive Number One."

I started a file that I called "Installation Instruction Number One: How we do things around here." But I realized that the "how" wasn't all I wanted to describe, and I drafted "Installation Instruction Number Two: What things we do around here."

I showed the two files to a few people but let the idea slide until, two years after our offsite, I met Dana's personnel manager, Mary Ann Cocke. She was enthusiastic about McPherson's one-pager and agreed to send me a copy.

Now I had three papers—the double-sided sheet from Dana plus the two instructions I had started to draft. I modeled my directive on Dana's, first just substituting words like "DOD" or "defense" for "Dana" or "automotive." It was a start, but I wasn't getting anywhere very fast. Gerry Kauvar offered to take a crack at it, and his version was much better than anything I had drafted. I took Gerry's version and started to work it over and over, with help from Doug Farbrother and Colonel Myles Caggins, my military assistant. Another director, Steve Joyce, suggested that what we needed wasn't so much a directive as a statement of principles, and he suggested the name that stuck: "Principles of Excellent Installations." One last change remained. Major General Jud Ellis, the TAC engineer and an example of unjustifiable overcommitment if ever there was one, took his black pen and started crossing out words until the principles fit on a wallet-size card.

In July 1985, two months after I had met Mary Ann Cocke and twenty-six months after our offsite, I mailed out 200 of the cards to senior defense leaders I knew. I told them to let me know if they wanted to help me spread the principles around, and I'd send them more cards.

I wasn't prepared for the response—within a month I had fifty-three requests, including eight from four-star generals and six from three-star generals, totaling 12,000 cards. My favorite response was—not surprisingly—General Welch's: "Send cards—lots!"

Myles Caggins got a few thousand postcards printed. One side bore our address, along with an unauthorized copy of a prepaid stamp. On the other side was printed, "I endorse the Principles of Excellent Installations. Please send my team member card to _____," and there was a place to fill in the address and to sign. People who signed up received a parchment copy of the Principles (see the appendix herein) and a gold wallet-size "Team Member" card with a short version of the principles.

I spent most of my remaining time at DOD running a direct mail operation. I sent a personal letter to every new base commander and to every military officer, colonel, or above, who was selected for promotion, congratulating them, inviting them to sign up for the Excellent Installations Team, offering my help, and wishing them "lots of luck and fun" in their new job.

Nearly every recipient signed up. In six years, we had 15,000 team members—people who had endorsed the principles. I could never have gotten that kind of a response with a directive.

Fortunately, it didn't have to be either/or. Will Taft, the deputy secretary of defense, was a true believer in deregulation and a passionate supporter of MIP. He adopted it as *his* program, and I reinforced this feeling in whatever way I could. We even got him his own model installation flag—just like the ones we gave to the installations with their installation name on it, except Taft's had *all* the model installation names. He had the flag displayed in his office.

At meetings of the DCIMI he would pound his fist on the table and *demand* that the MIPs be quickly approved. He loved the stories of craziness defeated and initiative rewarded. MIP needed support from the comptroller's office, since it controlled the money and had a zillion rules and restrictions that the commanders wanted waived. They were decently cooperative, if not enthusiastic. One of my counterparts in the comptroller's office told me, after I thanked him for approving a commander's waiver request, "Don't think I'm doing this because I believe in it. I just don't want to get in trouble with Will Taft."

In November 1985, at a commanders' conference, I presented Taft with a new flag listing all the model installations, which by then numbered thirty-five. Taft looked at the flag and commented, "There's no room on the flag to put new names. We'll have to find a new way to deregulate."

Taft wanted to extend the lessons we'd learned from the model installations to all of DOD. He had told the commanders that the only difference between model installations and the others was the way they were treated by headquarters. Now he wanted to treat all installations the same way.

It was finally our chance to adopt DOD Directive Number One. We prepared a one-page directive on installation management. It stated (in full):

1. The Commanding Officer of an installation is responsible for accomplishing the mission assigned to the installation, and should be delegated broad authority to decode how best to accomplish the mission, and is accountable for all resources applied to the mission.
2. Headquarters staff activities shall be directed toward facilitating any installation commander's ability to accomplish the mission. Regulations that limit installation commanders' freedom to do their jobs are contrary to the basic installation management policy, and shall be canceled or revised. Exceptions should be rare.
3. Except where required to preserve essential wartime support capability, or constrained by law or federal regulation,[8] installation commanders shall be free to purchase goods and services wherever they can get the combination of quality, responsiveness, and cost that best satisfies their requirements.
4. Unless prohibited by law, a share of any resources saved at an installation should be made available to the installation commander to improve the operations and working and living conditions at the installation.

We took it to the DOD Directives office (the same one that I had clashed with over the little yellow book), where we were told that it had to be numbered to fit their xxxx.x numbering system. George Schlossberg, my innovative lawyer, proposed DOD Directive Number 0001.0, but that didn't fly. I sent it to Taft for a signature, recommending that it be called, for effect, DOD Directive Number One. The late Donald O. "Doc" Cooke, the legendary mayor of the Pentagon and custodian of all directives, countered that the 4000-series was allocated to Installations and Logistics. Taft decided to call it DOD Directive Number 4001.1, and said to consider the number a symbol of how much further we needed to go.

I was disappointed with the number, but the commanders weren't at all disappointed with the result. I taught the directive personally to all the attendees at the services' training courses for new base commanders and got them to memorize my abbreviated version:

1. The commander is in charge.
2. Headquarters' job is to help.
3. Commanders can purchase goods and services wherever.
4. The base is entitled to share any money saved or earned.

They called it the base commanders' Bill of Rights. I'd bet that it was the only DOD directive that was ever widely memorized.

I began this chapter by saying the private sector has it all over government when it comes to management. I still think that's true, but it needn't be that way. *In Search of Excellence* highlighted the best practices of the private sector. MIP showed that similar practices could work in defense. At the same time I was applying *In Search of Excellence* in defense, executives were doing the same thing at other levels of government. Babak Armajani at the Minnesota Department of Administration and Ellen Schall at New York City's Department of Juvenile Justice in the 1980s used the same implementation model that we did: read the book, take the leadership offsite to figure it out, change everything. Other government executives told of similar experiences; for example, Bob O'Neill, Hampton, Virginia, city manager; Buddy McKay, Florida lieutenant governor; and David Couper, Madison, Wisconsin, police chief, who created an experimental police district that was a conceptual twin of MIP.

There are debates over whether government can be run like a business, but the debaters miss the point. Both government and business involve organizing and leading large numbers of people. The people are the same—they grew up in the same neighborhoods, went to the same schools, ate the same fast food; then some went to work in business, some in government. The same leadership and management tools are useful in both worlds. With inspired leadership, both groups are equally capable of excellence.

LESSONS FROM CHAPTER FOUR: TURNING AN ORGANIZATION AROUND

—Figure out what your organization should stand for: take your team offsite to figure it out together.

—Cultivate a "seemingly unjustifiable overcommitment" to what you stand for.

—Find examples to learn from and emulate in the private sector as well as the public.

—No more rules than you can put on a wallet-size card.

—Ball caps, T-shirts, stationery, lapel pins boost morale and commitment far beyond their cost.

—Build support for your plan by showing it personally to stakeholders and soliciting their advice and support—*before* you put it into action. Write to stakeholders and customers you can't visit.

NOTES

1. Thomas J. Peters and Robert W. Waterman, *In Search of Excellence* (New York: Harper & Row, 1982).

2. Peters and Waterman, *In Search of Excellence*, 157.

3. Peters and Waterman, *In Search of Excellence*, 164–165.

4. Peters and Waterman, *In Search of Excellence*, 146–147.

5. Frederick W. Taylor was the first "efficiency expert." He taught the world that there was "the one best way to do any work." See, for example, Robert Kanigel, *The One Best Way* (New York: Viking Books, 1997).

6. *Excellence in the Public Sector with Tom Peters*, Martin Sandler Productions (1989).

7. David Packard et al., *A Quest for Excellence, Final Report to the President,* The President's Blue Ribbon Commission on Defense Management (June 1986), xii.

8. These turned out to be overpowering exceptions.

5

Snakes and Snakebusters

(Dealing with Difficult Bosses)

In 1985, General Motors was a target of derision for the missionaries of the new management style. GM's market share had been eroded by Japanese imports, which were sexier, more reliable, and cheaper.

GM's new CEO, Roger Smith, seemed to understand the fix GM was in, and was committed to change. He made huge investments in new equipment, especially robots; he created Saturn, which was, as the commercials had it, "a new kind of car company"; and he entered into a joint venture with Toyota that converted the worst plant in all of GM into the maker of the highest quality cars in the world. I fancied myself in a position something like Smith's, trying to change a huge organization—I admired Smith and sympathized with him.

So I wasn't unhappy when in 1985, Bob Costello, a senior purchasing executive from GM, became assistant secretary of defense for procurement and logistics, and thus my new boss.

It was a fluke that I was working for the procurement chief. There had recently been a number of botched new weapon acquisitions, along with criminal scandals in which defense officials had taken bribes to influence contract awards. Congress decided that DOD needed an acquisition "czar," and split my parent organization—personnel and logistics—into a personnel piece and an acquisition piece. The installations organization, dealing as it did with working and living conditions for the troops and with services on military bases, was to be a part of the personnel piece.

To head the new acquisition piece, Secretary of Defense Caspar Weinberger turned to his old friend from his days at the Bechtel Corporation, Dick Godwin. Godwin was new to the defense world, but he knew construction from his years at Bechtel. In his introductory meeting on the organization of OSD, he saw that the installations office was to go with personnel. He asked whether "installations" included military construction. When he learned that it did, he told Weinberger that he wanted it in his organization, since it was the one part of DOD that he knew something about.

Too bad for me. And for the base commanders who were my customers. And for the troops they took care of. For the rest of my time at DOD, eight years, I was to report to a series of bosses whose world turned on issues of weapon development and procurement, not quality of life for the troops or local authority to run bases.

First there was Bob Costello. Costello, now deceased, introduced himself to me as "Roger Smith's change agent." In his first staff meeting he gave what he called his "checkers/workers" speech, which he used to illustrate why he was on the side of the workers. If that wasn't enough to make me love him, he cheerfully told everybody he met the story of the GM–Toyota joint venture, New United Motor Manufacturing Incorporated, or NUMMI.

GM had been assembling cars at its huge plant in Fremont, California, for many years. Around 1980, losing market share and having lost its reputation for quality, GM decided to close the Fremont plant, which was its least productive plant with the worst quality, worst absentee rate, and worst labor relations. Then Toyota, gaining market share and with the highest quality cars around, offered to take over the plant, sharing production with GM.

In 1980, Japanese car quality had become a metaphor for all the ways Japan was superior in the global competition. Schools were better, the culture was more suited to large business enterprise, the people were thriftier, and as a result, the workers were far better than American workers. So went the conventional wisdom.

Then came NUMMI. In a matter of months, the plant was producing the world's most reliable cars—Chevrolet Novas and Toyota Corollas, absolutely identical except for the nameplate. Fremont hadn't been failing because of the inferior American workers, after all. The same workers, members of the same local of the same United Auto Workers union, went from producing the worst cars in America to producing the best cars in the world.

The only thing that had changed was the management.

Costello summed it up with a story. He had visited the plant and asked a veteran forklift operator how things had changed.

"When you GM guys ran the plant you told me exactly when to deliver exactly what parts and exactly where to get them and exactly where to put them," she explained. "When Toyota came in they told me, 'This is *your* forklift and those are *your* parts. Your job is to use *your* forklift to get *your* parts to the assembly line as they are needed.' I'm working harder, I'm thinking harder, and I love it."

I could almost hear the words of Bill Creech—pilots with red scarves flying airplanes with red tails maintained by mechanics in red hats. How could I not love Bob Costello?

I briefed him on the principles of excellent installations, and he signed up on the spot. I told him about MIP and invited him to see for himself. That turned out to be the first of many big mistakes I made with Costello.

He immediately accepted my invitation, and within three weeks I escorted him to two of my favorites, the Marine Corps base at Camp Lejeune, North Carolina, and Moody Air Force Base in Valdosta, Georgia, the very first model installation nominated three years before by General Creech.

He was taken with the enthusiasm and innovative spirit we saw everywhere at the two bases. The workers, both military and civilian, felt empowered and special. MIP fit right in, I thought, with his admiration for NUMMI and with his checkers/workers speech.

But he didn't like the idea of giving some bases special treatment, and he directed me to stop. I thought that would gravely weaken the program, since the feeling of being special fueled the enthusiasm at the model installations. Deputy Secretary of Defense Will Taft had just weeks before signed the directive establishing the base commanders' "bill of rights," so any base could be a model installation if the commander wanted, and could get "special" treatment from OSD. The treatment wasn't really special, of course; it just meant that we would jump when any base commander asked for help with the bureaucracy.

Costello wanted me to stop providing ad hoc help and instead change the system. I explained that we could waive an inhibiting rule in a few days, compared to the months or years it would take to change or eliminate it, but he insisted that my job was to administer the system and change it when necessary, and not continue to preside over the granting of thousands (literally) of ad hoc waivers. I agreed, cheerfully, to do what he said.

I hoped that my quick agreement would help get his support for some other initiatives, starting with my plan to promote Pat Fowler. Pat was a fanatic about excellence, and I had recently appointed her director of customer service, a new, and until then unimaginable, title at DOD. I wanted to promote her to the senior executive service, or SES, the highest civilian rank in government. This would loudly symbolize, I believed, the new commitment to customer service in defense management.

"Are you nuts?" he exploded. "You want to use a precious SES billet on a director of *customer service?*" He was incredulous, and when he recovered his composure he took the billet away from installations so he could hire another procurement specialist.

The concept of serving customers was to cause me a great deal of grief with Costello and with most (thank goodness not all!) of my future bosses. It was a problem that many civil servants face: I wanted to serve my customers, who I had recognized were the base commanders, so that they could serve *their* customers, the soldiers, sailors, marines, and airmen who defend America. My bosses mostly had the—to me—unreasonable idea that I was there to serve *them.*

But I was often away from the office. To get to know what my customers wanted I was doing a lot of traveling. I found it exhilarating; so much so that my escorts from the military, usually midlevel officers fifteen years younger than I and in fighting trim condition, had a hard time keeping up with my pace.

A typical trip for me was the week of January 13, 1986: up at dawn on Monday to get a 7 A.M. flight on a T39 eight-passenger military jet from Andrews Air Force Base in Maryland to Pensacola Naval Training Center (Florida), where I met with the three-star admiral who headed all Navy training. Then back on the T39 to fly to Keesler Air Force Base in Gulfport, Mississippi, to meet the commander of that model installation and to tour the base and learn of the problems and opportunities he faced. Then on to Fort Polk, Louisiana, another model installation, where I stayed overnight in the base hotel.

Tuesday morning, up before dawn to breakfast with the troops, then a base tour, then on to Tulsa, Oklahoma, where the Army Corps of Engineers had a model engineer district (a MIP spin-off). Then a quick flight to Oklahoma City to see the Corps' handiwork in taking care of their customer, the huge Oklahoma City Air Logistics Center, which had been devastated by a fire and had to be rebuilt in a big hurry. After a tour of the logistics center, a night's sleep, then back on the plane early Wednesday to fly to Dallas to visit the Army & Air Force Exchange Service, Air Training Command headquarters at Randolph Air Force Base, and the Air Force Commissary Service.

Thursday morning I breakfasted with the Air Force regional civil engineer in Dallas, then back on the plane to spend the day at Fort Hood, a huge Army model installation near Killeen, Texas, commanded by then-Lieutenant General Crosbie (Butch) Saint, a bold and innovative commander who was one of my most enthusiastic supporters.[1] Then back on the plane to Fort Leavenworth, Kansas, for dinner and a quick tour before bed, then up Friday to lecture at the Army's command and general staff college. Then home.

I felt all right about being away from the office so much. I always left Doug Farbrother in charge, and he could run the organization and advise the boss at least as well as I. My trips, aside from being exciting, educational, and inspirational to me, made an important statement to commanders and staff alike about my priorities. I was following the old quality management axiom, "Watch my feet, not my mouth."

Unfortunately, many of my bosses were less than enthusiastic about where my feet were taking me. Not only wasn't I at hand in case they needed me, but when I returned I usually had a new list of things to do, new customers who needed help, and even less patience with the bureaucracy.

My customers weren't all that popular in the Pentagon. It's not widely understood that military people fall into two broad categories, staff and line. The staff includes engineers, supply specialists, buyers, doctors, chaplains, and so on. The line includes the main warfighting occupations: infantry, artillery, aviation, ship operations, and the like. Line officers tend to try to avoid Pentagon duty, because the work they love, along with promotion opportunities, are with the troops. They tend to favor decentralization and deregulation. Staff officers, on the other hand, gravitate to the Pentagon, which, after all, is the staff of all staffs. They're much more likely to favor centralization as well as regulations based on expertise; i.e., the "one best way."

Senior Pentagon officials are usually assigned a military officer as an executive assistant, and these officers are disproportionately from the staff corps—specialists who have mastered the rules of supply, engineering, and procurement. They are—often unfairly—looked down on by the line, from which nearly all base commanders are appointed. They are widely referred to as "staff weenies" who care more for their rules and regulations than for the mission of the base or unit. And in fact, they are much more likely than line officers to be sympathetic to the rules.

And they are likely to be suspicious of a defense official who supports base commanders. I was once briefing a boss on my goal of getting more authority to commanders, when he was warned off by his military assistant, a colonel who had been a supply specialist. "If you let Bob tell the commanders about his goals they'll love it, and then we'll have to do it."

Costello's military assistant was also a supply officer and no fan of line commanders. To make things worse, Costello himself had served in the Navy Reserve as a civil engineering officer, a member of the staff specialty that had created the largest part of the rules that commanders were calling on me to waive or cancel.

When it was time to issue the little yellow book I didn't think I'd get much sympathy from him. But since I had the authority under DOD to issue it on my own I went ahead without mentioning it to him. It was just another of hundreds of actions I took without my boss's involvement. In chapter 2, I described the ensuing brouhaha with Costello.

The yellow book doomed our relationship. From then on it seemed that the whole installations organization was under siege. I had approved Doug Farbrother's brilliant innovation to create two offices, one in Atlanta and one in Sacramento, whose only function was to help base commanders. They were called "installations assistance offices." Nothing remotely like them existed anywhere in DOD. They each employed four or five people who spent all their time on the road preaching the gospel of excellent installations and helping base commanders with a variety of issues they might have with the Pentagon.

To show Costello how much value they added to DOD I invited him to go along on "assistance visits" to a couple of bases. That ended badly. He visited the naval station at San Diego, where one of my heroes, a retired Marine sergeant named Bob Pruit, had taken over the "Scuttlebutt," a club for the lowest ranking sailors, and transformed it into a place where they could enjoy royal treatment, whether for a meal, billiards, darts, a family party, or anything they might do in their spare time. Pruit's club even made a profit. It was a great example of "unjustifiable overcommitment" and excellence.

Unfortunately, Pruit finished off Costello's tour at his "wall of honor," a display case showing off all the awards the Scuttlebutt had won. There in the center, surrounded by awards for the best club in the Pacific region and best club in the whole Navy, he proudly showed Costello "the one I prize the most, the Bob Stone award." It was just a bronze coin with the excellent installations seal on one side, and "Thanks, Bob Stone" in my handwriting on the other side. I had had the coins made on a recent trip to visit bases in Korea. They cost ninety cents each, and they made a nice award to hand out when I saw an example of excellence.

I never dreamed that the coins would get me in hot water and criticized for encouraging a "goddamn cult of personality."

Costello, egged on by his military assistant, decided I needed to be taught who I worked for, and it wasn't base commanders: it was him. He ordered me to cut way back on my visits to the field, and to drastically reduce the amount of travel of the installations assistance offices, which had been created *solely* to visit bases and help. To top it all off, he informed me that he was going to disestablish the assistance offices, my chief connection to my customers in the field.

I wasn't in love with Costello any more. More than my personal discomfort, what bothered me most was that he was strangling my ability to help base commanders, and through them, the troops. The real problem wasn't so much Costello; it was that the installations organization belonged in the personnel and readiness part of OSD, not in the acquisition part.

Perhaps I could secede.

On my theory that I could get anyone to pay attention to me for twenty seconds, I crafted a twenty-second speech to make to the assistant secretary for personnel and readiness, Grant Green. Grant was a retired Army infantry officer who was devoted to the troops, and also to *his* troops, i.e., his subordinates. I wanted to work for Grant, and I went to see him with my twenty-second speech.

"I'm a prisoner in a procurement factory. The installations organization doesn't belong in acquisition, it belongs with you. How about I just start reporting to you and sending all my memos through you?"

Grant laughed heartily, and gave me some sympathy, but my proposed secession didn't fit with his way of doing business. I was not going anywhere.

About that time I read about another leader who had become disillusioned with GM—Ross Perot. I had been an admirer of Perot's from reading about how he worked to free two employees of EDS from an Iranian jail. He had hired a team to go to Iran; then he fiercely protected them from EDS headquarters people who wanted to interfere. Surely if Perot were in the Pentagon he would be as fierce an advocate of base commanders' authority as I.

Fortune magazine ran an interview with Perot about his short experience as a member of the GM organization. Perot summed up the difference between the GM culture and EDS:

> At EDS if somebody sees a snake they kill it. At GM if somebody sees a snake they call a meeting to form a committee on snakes.

Gerry Kauvar had a habit of stewing when he was unhappy and concocting some wild entertainment that would get us all laughing at our troubles. This time he outdid himself. He created a board game called "Snakebusters."

The game was for two players. The object was to collect snakes while following a path, moving a number of spaces according to the roll of two dice.

One player followed a path called "The American Way." It was straight and led directly to the finish. The other path, labeled "The Pentagon Way," was tortuous, doubled back on itself, and contained chutes (no ladders) that, if you landed on one, would slide you back several moves.

Along the way there were "Chance" squares. A Chance card for the American player might read, "You sell a new idea. Collect $2 billion." A Chance card for the Pentagon player might read, "You saved money but the comptroller took it to pay for a weapon cost overrun, pay $10 billion."

Gerry had printed Snakebuster money—one- and ten-billion-dollar bills he had made from photocopied one-dollar bills with Bozo the Clown's face scanned in over George Washington's. Snakes were candy "Gummi Worms."

Fearless and, I thought, a little rash, Gerry had brought the game to my Pentagon office, where he demonstrated it to Doug Farbrother and me. We were all falling-down laughing, but when we finished I told Gerry privately to take the game home and never to bring it to the Pentagon. We had an offsite planning session scheduled soon after that, and Gerry brought the game and all the installations directors played it, amid much hilarity. It brought a much-needed lift to our morale.

John Gardner once said, "The first task of a leader is to keep hope alive." Snakebusters and the defiant attitude it signaled helped keep our hope alive.

One of the realities about government service is that bosses move on. In the fall of 1987, less than a year after Costello became assistant secretary, his boss, Dick Godwin, announced his resignation as undersecretary for acquisition, and Costello was nominated to succeed him. I was thrilled: as undersecretary for acquisition, he would be far too busy with important matters—like acquiring the latest fighter plane—to worry about the likes of me and my team. I was right—in the year he was undersecretary I saw him only twice, and once was at his going away party.

Costello was succeeded by Jack Katzen, who supported my efforts while taking care to avoid getting crosswise with Costello—his boss. There was only a year left in the Reagan administration, and it was time to start getting ready for the new team, whoever it might be.

I started to put together a proposal for the incoming secretary of defense. I called it *The Authority Book*, and its main message—indeed its *only* message—was that defense capability could be increased dramatically if the new secretary personally made it a priority to decentralize authority from the Pentagon and other headquarters to commanders in the field.

Secretaries Weinberger and Carlucci had both been believers in supporting the field commanders. In fact, Carlucci and his deputy, Will Taft, had signed directives establishing total quality management and the model installation management approach as DOD-wide policy, and Taft talked often about the need to deregulate DOD operations. They had all helped move DOD in the right direction. But I believed that the issue of authority was still *the* most important issue in defense management, and warranted a major part of the personal time and effort of the secretary of defense.

I worked through the summer and fall to sharpen and polish *The Authority Book*, with a lot of help from my colleagues and customers, including many of America's top military leaders. I finally had a product that had the endorsement of—among many others—Chairman of the Joint Chiefs of Staff Colin Powell, Air Force Chief Larry Welch, and Central Command CINC H. Norman Schwartzkopf, along with David Packard, who was widely revered as an expert on how to strengthen defense.

All I needed now was a way to get it to the new secretary. After the 1988 election, President-elect Bush announced that he would nominate Senator John Tower, ranking Republican and former chairman of the Senate Armed Services Committee to the position of secretary of defense. Although not yet confirmed by the Senate, Tower followed a long tradition of defense secretaries by traveling to Germany to attend the Wehrkunde conference of top international defense people. One of my best customers, Air Force Brigadier General Buster Glosson, a former commander of the first model installation (and future planner of the air war over Iraq), was assigned to accompany Tower to Germany.

Buster took *The Authority Book* with him, and on the long flight home got Tower to read it. Tower wrote in the margin, next to the specific actions I recommended, "I really *really* like this."

Too bad for my plan that the Senate would reject Tower's nomination. Soon Dick Cheney was nominated and confirmed as secretary of defense, and I had no way to get to him except through channels, i.e., through my boss, Jack Katzen, who continued as assistant secretary until Cheney's appointee, Colin McMillan, was confirmed.

I took Katzen *The Authority Book*, and to my relief he liked it. But he refused to endorse it to Cheney, saying that of course Cheney already knew all that. And I put *The Authority Book* away for four years, until 1993, when I would do my best to put it into effect across the government.

But meanwhile there was yet another new boss. Colin McMillan was an independent oil producer and chili pepper farmer who had managed George

Bush's campaign in New Mexico. He was a decent and capable person, but unfortunately it took me only two weeks to get crosswise with him.

One of his first ideas was to centralize all of DOD's commissary operations. Each of the four services had long run its own system of commissaries—grocery stores on military bases that were heavily subsidized and sold groceries and sundries to the troops (and retirees) for about twenty-five percent less than civilian supermarkets.

McMillan proposed, and the deputy secretary of defense had approved, replacing the four commissary organizations with a single defense agency (where had I heard *that* idea before!) to eliminate duplication and save money.

By now I was deeply, fanatically opposed to centralization, and especially to one that would take operations away from the military departments and move them to OSD, which was a giant step more removed from the troops. So when McMillan asked my help in managing the consolidation I explained that it was a terrible idea—not what he wanted to hear.

He did let me pursue an alternative. I pointed out that there already was an excellent commissary organization, the Air Force Commissary Service. If there had to be a single commissary organization, why not turn the whole job over to the Air Force, allowing it to take over the existing Army, Navy, and Marine Corps stores and headquarters.

McMillan would consider it if I could get the services to agree. The Army and Marine Corps generals I worked with reluctantly agreed that they would probably be better off with the Air Force than with a brand new defense agency run by OSD.

But the Navy admiral responsible for commissary policy was passionately and unalterably opposed. "IF THE AIR FORCE TAKES OVER THEY'LL CLOSE THE NORFOLK COMMISSARY AND MAKE THE SAILORS HITCHHIKE TO LANGLEY! [an Air Force Base ten miles from the huge navy complex at Norfolk]," he screamed at me. And so my counterproposal was dead. DOD got a new defense agency, the military departments lost control over the commissary stores,[2] and my relationship with McMillan was damaged and would remain so for his remaining three years.

The low point came shortly after he attended one of my base commanders conferences and was badgered by several of the commanders about the latest management initiatives and about the general proclivity of OSD to take authority away from commanders. McMillan saw the commanders as agents for the status quo, and angrily ordered me to immediately stop sponsoring commanders' conferences and disband the installation assistance offices that held them.

By the end of the Bush administration I had had a string of bad luck with bosses (except for Jack Katzen), and a string of bosses most assuredly figured they had bad luck with me.[3]

What was the problem, and how could it have been avoided? How might I have dealt with difficult bosses? And how might they have dealt with somebody like me?

First, me. I had a job to do and I was doing it the best way I knew. I had lots of signals that I was going about it right, from enthusiastic approval of DOD leaders like Secretary Carlucci and Deputy Secretary Taft to support from senior military leaders of all services, to a featured segment on Tom Peters' TV special, *Excellence in the Public Sector*. My management and leadership techniques had become a part of me. I wasn't going to change.

And my bosses? They had accepted assistant secretary appointments at big cuts in income and independence because they wanted to make a difference. It would have been nice if they had said to the senior staffs they inherited, "You're doing great. Just keep on doing what you've been doing."

But that couldn't have happened either. They didn't join up to endorse the status quo. Nor should they have—there was always much that needed changing.

While I couldn't change, and my new bosses couldn't say "keep it up," there was one thing they could have done. Only Larry Korb had done it. They could have moved me to a different position.

When Korb came in as assistant secretary in 1981 he wanted to make big changes in installations (just a part of his responsibility, which included manpower, reserve affairs, and logistics), and so he had strong-armed me into moving into the installations job, as I explained in chapter 2.

Had he not moved me I would have continued to do my previous job—managing budgeting and congressional testimony for the organization—the same way as I had been doing. Korb would probably have been unhappy with my performance because I would have likely been defending the positions the organization had taken in the Carter administration, and the Reagan Pentagon had decidedly different priorities and methods.

By moving me Korb got a twofer: he got me to take a fresh look at installations management, and he got his own person to take a fresh look at my old job.

And by moving, I got a great new opportunity to learn and to make big changes. And I got the chance to grow as a leader. Looking back on the eight years I spent as deputy assistant secretary of defense for Installations, I'd judge that my most effective years were probably the middle ones—years three through six. After that the job was routine for me.

This may be a characteristic of many fields of endeavor. It's widely known that most Nobel Prize-winning scientists win for work done early in their careers. The definitive study of performance of major league baseball managers shows that "A huge percentage of managers have their best seasons when they first get a chance to manage and in their first years on a new job."[4]

Moving executives is not common in the federal government. It should be. Five years in one job is enough for any executive.

The law establishing the Senior Executive Service explicitly provided for members of the SES to be mobile—i.e., to change jobs frequently. James Lee Witt, the administrator of the Federal Emergency Management Agency (FEMA) from 1993 to 2001, led what was arguably the most successful turnaround in government since Bill Creech's transformation of TAC in the early 1980s. Witt credits much of his success to his moving every senior executive he inherited to a new job in FEMA.

In my case, it certainly worked for the one boss who tried it. The ones who didn't move me missed big opportunities for twofers.

But a much bigger move still lay ahead for me: the move from DOD to the White House and Al Gore's project to reinvent the entire federal government.

LESSONS FROM CHAPTER FIVE: DEALING WITH DIFFICULT BOSSES

—Never fall in love at first sight with the boss. Love needs to be earned and reciprocated.

—Be cautious about inviting your new boss into the details of your business.

—Try to shield your team from a difficult new boss. Your main job is to keep hope alive.

—If you've been in your job for more than a couple of years, volunteer to move to a new one when a new boss comes in.

—It really is easier to get forgiveness than permission. But not always.

NOTES

1. Butch Saint's name isn't known widely outside the military, but it should be. In 1990, as army commander in Europe, he was responsible for one of the most amazing achievements in military history: in just a few weeks he moved VII Corps, 100,000-strong and designed to remain in place forever defending half of the American front in Germany against a possible Soviet attack, from dozens of bases and camps in Germany to Saudi Arabia, where it arrived, rolled off hundreds of cargo ships and into battle, where it won the war against Iraqi forces.

2. The commissary consolidation, unlike most consolidations, worked out better in practice than in theory: operating costs and prices to customers were reduced, and customer satisfaction increased.

3. McMillan now generously denies that I was bad luck for him: He wrote me, "While I did not agree with your philosophy in many areas, I thought you were an excellent administrator."

4. Bill James, *The Bill James Guide to Baseball Managers from 1870 to Today* (New York: Scribner, 1997), 155.

Getting to Reinvention

(Seizing the Chance of a Lifetime)

Flying to California in 1985, I ran out of reading material on the plane; I picked up a copy of *Inc.* magazine and paged through it. On page fifty-four was "The Most Entrepreneurial City in America," an article about Visalia, California, and its city manager, Ted Gaebler, who was introducing innovation and competition to city services—just what I was trying to get base commanders to do.

I was sponsoring an upcoming conference of base commanders, and I thought Ted would be a natural, so I made sure he was invited to speak. Unfortunately, I had to miss the conference, but I didn't want to miss the chance to meet Ted; I invited him to visit me at the Pentagon.

He showed up with David Osborne, the author of the *Inc.* article and his collaborator on a just-started book. Our conversation went on and on, soon turning into a monologue as they listened deeply to my stories and experiences. They left with all my "Excellent Installations" paraphernalia—the fake-parchment certificate with the principles, an (unauthorized) postage-free post card to join the Excellent Installations team, a gold plastic card with the summarized principles, lapel pins, and even a pair of Excellent Installations cuff links.

Ted soon left Visalia and started consulting. He called one day to tell me that he was using my experiences to encourage state government people in Oregon. "I tell them if the Pentagon can change, then surely they can change in Eugene."

David and Ted told me they would include my story in their book, but I was flabbergasted when their best-selling *Reinventing Government* was published, and I saw how extensively they had used my experience—nine citations in the index, with two of them referring to three-page stories. I was famous—or rather notorious—in the Pentagon, especially after *Newsweek* ran a special section with a ten-page extract that prominently featured my claim that the Pentagon wasted $100 billion per year through foolish over-regulation.

Bill Clinton, then governor of Arkansas, received only two mentions (but who's counting) in *Reinventing Government*, but he was a true believer. One day in March 1992, I was electrified to see an interview with him in *USA Today* in which he spoke knowledgeably about reinventing government and about how that was going to be high on his agenda if elected president later that year.

That got me scheming with David Osborne (a fellow at the Progressive Policy Institute, the New Democrat think tank) about how I could be a part of reinventing government if Clinton was elected. David was an insider who spent time in Little Rock and in meetings with the Clinton brain trust.

The election came and went—Clinton won—but the reinvention front was quiet. I read everything I could get my hands on, watched C-SPAN coverage of the Clinton preparations, and called David almost daily. Nothing seemed to be happening.

I took the opportunity to meet several people at David's suggestion—Bob Knisely, acting director of the Bureau of Transportation Statistics—as obscure an organization as there was in the whole government; and John Kamensky, a staff member of the GAO. Bob had held about twenty different jobs in government and knew a great deal about how the whole government worked, while John had spent several months at GAO studying and visiting the governments of New Zealand, Australia, and the United Kingdom, which were the pioneers in a soon-to-be burgeoning worldwide reform movement, one the United States hadn't yet joined.

Suddenly, disaster! On March 3, 1993, Clinton held a press conference announcing his reinventing government initiative—no mention of the need to eliminate over-regulation, to empower employees, and to serve customers. Instead, his announcement might have been made by any of his predecessors. Reinventing government was apparently to be another waste-finding exercise involving the comptrollers and, especially, the IGs. It was to be called the National Performance Review (NPR) and was to be modeled after the Texas Performance Review. It was to be headed by Vice President Al Gore. I searched the crowd around Clinton for a sign of David Osborne. Nothing. My dreams of reinvention seemed dead.

Two days later, I returned to my office from a meeting to find a telephone message: Call Elaine Kamarck in the office of the vice president. Hope was back.

The next day I went to Elaine's office in the Eisenhower (Old) Executive Office Building, a 120-year-old French Empire masterpiece that had housed the Departments of State, War, and Navy in the nineteenth century and that now housed most of the White House staff. Kamensky and Knisely were there, and Elaine quizzed us on what was wrong with government and how to fix it. After just a few minutes she exclaimed, "Jesus! Gore's gotta hear this!"

In another minute, we were on the vice president's calendar for a two-hour meeting set for the coming Sunday, March 14, 1993.

Elaine told me later how our meeting had come about. She had known Clinton as a colleague in the Democratic Leadership Council (DLC) and had expected his administration to be heavily staffed with DLC people. But all through the transition period and into February only one DLC member joined the White House staff. Elaine wrote in her *Newsday* column that Clinton had apparently abandoned his New Democrat friends; she was promptly called to the White House and offered the job as senior policy advisor to the vice president—whom she hadn't known before. She expected that Gore and she would work on welfare reform, which they both knew a lot about and which had been a central part of the Clinton campaign: "End welfare as we know it."

Her second day on the job she got a call from the vice president.

"Know anything about reinventing government?" he asked, before telling her of their new assignment.

"No, but I know the guy who wrote the book," she replied.

Frantic, she called David Osborne. "David, what do we do?"

He had the answer. "Talk to Stone, Knisely, and Kamensky." Hence, our invitation.

The day before our scheduled Sunday meeting with the vice president, Washington was hit with a late winter snowstorm, and I feared our meeting would be called on account of weather, never to be rescheduled. If it was going to be called off, it wouldn't be because the three of us couldn't make it: Knisely had a four-wheel drive vehicle that he used to bring Kamensky over to my house to prepare for our big chance.

We planned to meet for a couple of hours, but we got so excited exchanging stories that it wasn't until Roxane, my wife, brought us a pizza six hours later that we had any concept of what time it was. We divvied up our presentations. Kamensky would talk about government reform around the world. Knisely would talk about his concept of *program design*—the idea that government programs could be designed to work from the start and that this would make a difference. I was to talk about how the government really operated, explaining how the excessive centralization and over-regulation wreaked bureaucratic craziness on people who worked at military bases.

I would bring along a few of my "props"—my little yellow book; my can of commercial spray paint that had been "revalidated" by the base chemist at the Anniston, Alabama, Army Depot; and my favorite prop of all, my steam trap.

I had gotten the steam trap in the mail from the base engineer at the Sacramento Army Depot, along with a letter of explanation: a steam trap is a softball-sized plumbing fixture that removes water from steam lines. The letter explained that it costs about $100 and when it leaks, as steam traps eventually do, it can easily leak steam at a rate of $50 a week.

Unfortunately, the engineer who needed steam traps had no authority to buy anything. The system mistrusted everybody but specially trained procurement people to do the buying. Compounding the situation, procurement people were trained to save up small orders so they could make big buys at a discount. As a result, the procurement office had taken over a year to acquire the needed steam traps. Good news: they bought them at a discount of $10 each. Bad news: the wait had wasted steam worth more than $2,000 per steam trap.

Kamensky and Knisely loved the steam trap story. Knisely opined that Gore would probably want to keep the steam trap; if he let me leave with it, it would mean we had failed to persuade him that he needed our help to reinvent government.

One more item of preparation remained. Knisely raised the issue: what should we wear to a Sunday meeting with the vice president at the White House? He knew.

"I know how he'll think. I'm a preppie just like him—same background, St. Albans School, Harvard. He'll be wearing jeans and a sports jacket. That's what we should wear."

I had my doubts, so I went to Roxane for advice, as I always do.

"You've never worn a sports jacket with jeans in your life," she pointed out accurately. "You'd feel uncomfortable dressed like that. Wear what you wear to the office on weekends."

Sunday, March 14, 1993, dawned bright and cold. The snow had turned to ice, covering all the roads. Knisely picked us up in his four-wheel drive. Under our parkas, Kamensky and I wore casual slacks and sports jackets, Knisely, jeans and a sports jacket.

I was carrying a gym bag with all my props. I was alarmed when I saw I'd need to pass the bag through the White House x-ray machine. The steam trap would look like a bomb to the Secret Service man at the entrance. Apparently, the fact that I was on the list as having an appointment with the vice president allowed me to take in my bomb-sized package.

We waited in the White House west lobby, where we met the others who would attend the meeting with Gore: Phil Lader, friend of the president and deputy director of the Office of Management and Budget; his assistant, Margaret Yao; and Elaine Kamarck. We were all dressed casually. Elaine was in jeans.

Gore was late, and for a few minutes I worried that my chance of a lifetime would be called off. But soon we were escorted into Gore's West Wing office, and there he was, flesh and blood just like us.

He was wearing chinos and a flannel shirt. He made us feel at ease immediately with a mock complaint.

"This job! You can't even escape when you're snowed in. You know, the Secret Service has snowplows! And they come get you if you don't show up." He went on to explain how, in his wife's absence, he and "the other soccer moms" had been on the phone all morning trying to figure out what to do about their daughters who were stranded in Richmond after a soccer game.

Then he turned to Elaine, and she introduced her "team." Me first. I explained how good people were trapped in a bad system of centralization and over-regulation that kept them doing senseless things and kept them from achieving excellence. When I explained that in my job at the Pentagon I had little authority other than making speeches and writing letters, he exclaimed, "That sounds just like my job."

I laid out for him my formula for transforming a large organization:

1. Have a simple uplifting message that you repeat over and over and over. (Like "Excellent Installations, the Foundation of Defense.")
2. Get your message across through human stories and props that are easy to understand.
3. Praise people who are doing the right things, and don't waste one second going after waste, fraud, and abuse.

I showed him a reinventing government gold card, patterned after the Excellent Installations Team Member Gold Card, complete with his signature and Clinton's, copied and reproduced without permission. He smiled at that. I told him the story of the steam trap, the paint can, and the little yellow book. Then Knisely took over, explaining how the fall of the Soviet Union had left the U.S. government as the last bastion of communist management; then Kamensky explained how reinvention in New Zealand had blazed a trail that we could follow with little risk of failure.

Gore spent three hours with us, questioning us on everything we knew and listening with total concentration to our answers. Nearing the end of the meeting, I started to pack up my props. As I was putting the steam trap in my gym bag, he reached across the table and put his hand squarely on it.

"Any chance of your leaving that with me?" he asked. My heart skipped a beat. Then he said, "I'd like you all to come to work with me for six months on reinventing government. What do you say?"

"Yes!" said Knisely, "But you need to clear it with Peña [the secretary of transportation]."

"I'd like to, but I'll have to ask my boss," I said. "Do you have any influence with him?"

He allowed that he probably did, then turned to the third member of the team, John Kamensky.

"I'd like to, but I'll have to ask my wife," John said. The next day it was a done deal for all three of us. Tuesday I did the last piece of work I was ever to do for DOD: testify before the House Armed Services Committee on the third round of base closures.

Wednesday I showed up for duty at Elaine Kamarck's office where a big surprise was in store for me. There was a forty-eight by sixty-inch organization chart mounted on a foam board in Elaine's office, and at the very top was a box containing the words *Bob Stone, project director.*

It was unimaginable for a brand new administration to risk such an important (at least, it seemed very important to me) initiative by putting it in the hands of career employees, and Gore was advised not to. But he trusted us and would go on trusting us for all the years we worked for him.

Now we had to earn that trust.

LESSONS FROM CHAPTER SIX: SEIZING THE CHANCE OF A LIFETIME

—Network, even if it doesn't come naturally. (It didn't for me.) Connect with people who are fighting the battles you are, even if they're on distant fronts. It often pays off in completely unexpected ways.

—Find and use "props" to make your point. I captured people's imaginations with my steam trap, my little yellow book, and many others.

—When you get your chance, be natural, but prepare. "Natural" and "prepared" aren't mutually exclusive.

7

Hi Ho, Hi Ho,
It's Off to Work We Go

(Assembling a Team for a Big New Job)

I hadn't been kidding when I told Gore I would have to ask my boss if I could join him for six months. My previous boss, Bush appointee Colin McMillan, had returned to New Mexico after Clinton's election, and his deputy was left to run the show until the Clinton–Gore team was in place. I didn't have any reason to believe that the new boss would want to support me. I just hoped that, as a Republican appointee who was a holdover into the new administration, he would avoid any action that might compromise his chances of staying on.

He belonged to the management school that considers praise corrupting—certainly he had never uttered a word of praise or approval to me. And when he didn't get what he wanted, he could be abusive. Once he called me and got my voicemail. When I called him back a few minutes later, he was in a rage.

"If I ever get your voicemail again," he screamed, "I'll fire you."

I didn't think that was grounds for firing, but I took the threat seriously enough to have my voicemail disconnected the same day. Apparently he wasn't as infuriated by getting no answer.

I didn't want to repeat the mistake I had made with Bob Costello over the little yellow book—no surprises this time—so I had kept him informed about my meeting with Kamarck and her decision to have me brief Gore. I told him about the Gore meeting and invitation, and we agreed that I would do my scheduled Tuesday congressional testimony on the new base closure package, and then I could start work for Gore on Wednesday, March 17, 1993.

I spent Monday getting ready for the hearing, and testified Tuesday morning. Tuesday afternoon found me straightening out my office and going over loose ends with Captain Dick Marvin, my military assistant, and Gerry Kauvar, who I expected would serve as acting deputy assistant secretary of defense until I returned. Had I had any inkling that I would never return to the building where I had served for twenty-four years—and grown up in many ways— it would have been a sentimental occasion. As it was, my only emotion was excitement about going to the White House.[1]

On Wednesday morning, I showed up for work at Elaine Kamarck's office. I brought two people with me from the Pentagon: Doug Farbrother, my old sidekick, and Marv Voskuhl, an Air Force colonel and former base commander who combined brilliance with patience and would make a peerless administrative officer—a job not entirely unlike being a base commander.

Of course, we didn't have a base. For the time being, our base was the old beat-up sofa in Kamarck's office that we shared with Kamensky, Knisely, and, not least, Kamarck and all her visitors.

Voskuhl and I tried to figure out what we would need to deliver a report in six months on how to reinvent the entire government. We'd need people, offices, computers, phones, and money.

What we really needed first was Dick Feezle. Feezle was a long-time member of the staff of the OMB, fallen from grace but very wise in the ways of government and well connected to a handful of people who really ran the government, especially Doc Cooke at the Pentagon.

Feezle decided to help the vice president's team. Whether from a sense of what was right or a desire to thwart his OMB colleagues who had hoped to grab the reinvention job for themselves, or because he was blinded by Kamarck's glamour, I never knew; but helpful he was.

I had no clue about where we would set up shop and didn't even appreciate how important it would be to be very close to the White House. Feezle did, and he knew all the vacant offices that were under lease to the government's General Services Administration (GSA). He found two suites immediately: one a beat-up suite of offices nine blocks away on Vermont Avenue, the other a nice suite a block from the White House. Somebody else in the White House was planning to grab the nice place, but at Feezle's insistence, we got Gore to stake a claim on it.

The problem was, we had no money. GSA's operating method was to lease space, then sublease it to the government agencies that actually used it. We would have to beg for the space. Feezle found an obscure provision of the appropriations law that seemed to give GSA the authority to give us the building rent free, if they wanted. So Feezle asked for it.

The next day Dennis Fischer stuck his head in Elaine's doorway. Fischer was a veteran civil servant who was serving as acting administrator of GSA until the new administration's person could be nominated and confirmed.

"How serious are you about wanting that office space?" he asked Elaine. He was willing to give it to us under the authority that Feezle had found, but there was some risk involved to him and to GSA. The OMB staffer who controlled GSA's budget had threatened to slash it if Dennis gave us the building. Dennis was willing to take that chance, but only if Kamarck could assure him that the vice president's office really needed it.

"Damn fucking right we want it," Kamarck responded. We got the office space we needed. It was our first exposure to the extraordinary power and chutzpah of OMB staffers. They never feared to oppose the vice president, or anybody else, as long as they could do it anonymously. (To their credit, in later meetings with Gore, several were willing to argue vehemently with him to his face over reinvention issues.)

Money was easier. Another obscure provision of law, which Feezle ferreted out, prevented agencies from sharing the cost of a multiagency task force like the National Performance Review (NPR). One agency had to bear the entire cost, and Feezle chose DOD for the honor. He greased the way with Doc Cooke, and Kamarck asked Larry Smith, an old friend who was counselor to Les Aspin, secretary of defense, for the money.

Kamarck told me that DOD was so proud that one of their people, me, had been selected to run the show that they had agreed to fund us to the tune of $1.6 million. I later heard a different story from Doc Cooke.

I was at an awards ceremony two years later when Doc took my arm and introduced me to Bill Perry, who had replaced Aspin as secretary of defense.

"This is Bob Stone," he started. "I'm spending $1.3 million [the then-current amount] of your money to keep him across the river, far from the Pentagon, and it's a bargain at the price." Cooke roared with laughter at his joke, as he often did; I wasn't sure he was joking. Roxane paled when she heard the story. She was certain he wasn't joking. But with Doc you never knew.

Later Gore, repeating the story to me, dissolved into laughter.

"Doc's not joking," I protested.

"I know he's not," Gore replied, laughing even harder. I never quite got the joke, but we had our money.

Now we needed people, talented people who burned to reinvent government. I first invited Mike Serlin to join us. Serlin was an executive at the Treasury Department who was heading its Center for Applied Financial Management, an innovative and entrepreneurial outfit that he had started two years before. Mike was interested but hemmed and hawed, then turned me down, saying he just had too much to do and that the fledgling Center needed him. Then he stopped and was silent for a few seconds.

"No!" he blurted. "You know, back in 1963, I was at work in my office one day and a friend came in and said, 'Let's go down to the Mall and listen to Martin Luther King.' I told him I was too busy, and I missed one of the great experiences in American history. I'm not going to let that happen again. Count me in!!"

So we had another reinvention leader on the team. Fortunately, while I was trying to handpick a staff one person at a time, David Osborne and John Kamensky were systematically organizing the NPR into teams and poring over their Rolodexes for reinvention-minded people all over the government.

Also fortunately for me, Elaine had borrowed Billy Hamilton, deputy comptroller of the state of Texas, from the state comptroller, John Sharp, a colleague of hers from the Democratic Leadership Council. Sharp and Hamilton had led the Texas Performance Review, on which the president had modeled his expectation for the NPR. Hamilton joined the NPR as a deputy director and brought a group of energetic assistants with him. They sat for hours, answering the phone calls of federal employees who wanted to join the crusade, reviewing applications, and hiring people. They didn't seem to need my approval, so I stayed out of it. They hired practically everybody who applied, including IG staffers encouraged by the presidential announcement that had so depressed me, civil servants in hot water with their bosses who needed a safe haven for a while, and people who were sent to NPR as a fifth column, people who would defend the interests of their agencies against this latest reform effort.

Mostly they hired dedicated government employees who had struggled in the trenches or in headquarters to do a great job in spite of the bureaucracy that favored caution, process, and stasis. NPR also brought on board every Presidential Management Intern (PMI) we could find. PMIs were newly hired graduates of schools of public administration who were being rotated between assignments for a two-year development period before settling into their career assignments. Their lack of experience was far outweighed by their idealism, their youthful energy, and their impatience with a status quo to which they had barely been exposed.

We also brought in, to our huge benefit, fellows of the Council for Excellence in Government, midcareer feds in a leadership development program.

Some new political appointees helped us, too. Doug Ross joined the Labor Department from the University of Michigan and sent over two graduate students, Loriee Evans and Susan Moffitt, who he had brought to Washington with a promise of $300-a-week internships. When they showed up at Labor to get on the payroll, they were told there were no $300-a-week jobs possible: they would have to hire on as GS-3s earning $600 a week. That was their introduction to the crazy quilt of rules and regulations that typified the federal government in 1993.

Overall, I was astounded by the talents of the people who showed up to staff the NPR. I had expected a few high performers and a lot of untalented people. I had the proportions absolutely backward. We wound up with magnificently talented and dedicated people. When one of my recruiting efforts failed—I had tried very hard to get the Pentagon to lend us Joan Freeman, who had created a new kind of budgeting and financing for half the DOD, to lead our budget team—I resignedly elevated Beverly Godwin, a volunteer from the Department of Health and Human Services. Godwin did a great job, made a big hit with Gore, and served effectively at NPR for its entire eight-year run. So much for my recruiting instincts.

Leaders showed up, thanks mostly to Kamarck and David Osborne. Carolyn Lukensmeyer, previously chief of staff to Governor Dick Celeste of Ohio, joined the team as one of four deputy directors, along with Hamilton, Kamensky, and Knisely.

We organized into about thirty teams. About fifteen teams reviewed individual agencies. Fifteen others worked on government-wide issues—customer service, procurement, budget, personnel, quality leadership and management, and so on. The teams were assigned to produce recommendations to make government work better and cost less.

We now had the resources we needed to do our work: people, organization, an office, an assignment, a leadership team, and a budget. We were ready for the kickoff.

Elaine wanted Gore to give the team its formal charge. We got the biggest conference room in the White House complex and invited all of our new team to the official opening of NPR. Gore gave an inspiring address, telling the team that our job was to restore Americans' faith in government and redeem the promise of Philadelphia. David Osborne gave an uplifting lecture that told all assembled just what reinvention meant. The only down moment of the day was provided by Phil Lader, deputy director of OMB for management, who advised us not to set our sights too high. Quoting Peter Drucker, he warned, "You cannot defy gravity."

To give a closing motivational speech, the Texas team had brought in John Daly, a professor from the University of Texas. Daly was funny, provocative, and inspiring. He finished by getting the audience to stand at our seats and repeat after him, by section, some gibberish that ended up with half the assembly shouting "hi," then the other half shouting "ho." John got us all facing the exit and coaxed us into sounding "hi ho, hi ho," then he sang "It's off to work we go!"

The next day's *Washington Post* wrapped up its coverage of the event with this closing:

> He ended his remarks by discussing customer strategies used by the Disney Company and led the group in a refrain from *Snow White and the Seven Dwarfs*. And off to work they went.

LESSONS FROM CHAPTER SEVEN: ASSEMBLING A TEAM FOR A BIG NEW JOB

—Every team needs a Feezle—an old hand who knows how to get things done, through and around the bureaucracy.

—People are the most important asset, and people in an organization know best what's wrong and how to fix it.

—Youth and inexperience are precious assets. Make sure to include them.

—Make sure you have money and the right location—sometimes you want to be near the center of power, sometimes you want to be far from the center of interference.

NOTE

1. "Working at the White House" is an accepted Washington exaggeration. The West Wing of the White House, where the president works, is very small with very few offices—perhaps 200 people work there. Most of the White House staff works in the Eisenhower Executive Office Building—the ornate nineteenth-century architectural curiosity and treasure that Jacqueline Kennedy rescued from the wrecking ball in the 1960s. Some of the White House staff works across Lafayette Park in the nineteenth-century townhouses; others work in commercial buildings nearby (as I was to do). But the little exaggeration is universally accepted: "I work at the White House."

It's September 7th, Stupid!

(Getting a Big Job Done in a Hurry)

The NPR staff, suddenly very large, needed a home. When Dick Feezle had located space for us, I told Elaine Kamarck that we would need space for forty people—fifty tops—and we could fit them all in the office a block from the White House. Elaine wisely counseled me to glom onto the other space, nine blocks away on Vermont Avenue, as well.

It was good that she did, because we had a prolific recruiting operation. Besides the Texans hiring practically everybody who volunteered, David Osborne and John Kamensky recruited every federal employee they had found trying to reinvent. In addition, because relations with state and local governments were a central issue in NPR, David brought in civil servants from Hampton, Virginia; Phoenix, Arizona; Sunnyvale, California; and the Oregon state government. Before I knew it, we had 250 people. We squeezed about sixty into the nearby space, eighty into Vermont Avenue, and bunked out the rest in various government agencies.

I had to first decide who got the prime space close to the White House. My formula was simple: I put the teams that I had the most confidence in, or that knew best what they had to do, at Vermont Avenue. The others I put in the nearby space where I would naturally spend time with them.

I didn't want the Vermont Avenue folks to feel like outcasts or to be in the dark about what was going on in the White House, so I decided to hold twice-weekly staff meetings at the Vermont Avenue office. That contact still didn't seem enough to keep them in the loop on a project that was bound to be fast moving and always changing. One of our Council for Excellence in

Government fellows, Jean Logan, volunteered to serve as "town crier." Twice a day, after my 8:30 leadership meetings and in midafternoon, rain or shine, Jean traipsed the nine blocks to Vermont Avenue to announce to the eighty staffers what great new thing Elaine, Gore or I had cooked up in the last few hours.

Low tech, but an effective way of keeping everybody informed and up to the hour, if not to the minute.

I was very conscious of time. Clinton had asked Gore for a report by September 7, which was six months plus the Labor Day weekend from the March 3, 1993, announcement. I was determined to meet the deadline, whatever it took.

Elaine Kamarck had dubbed our conference room "The War Room," after the well-known room in Little Rock where the 1992 Clinton–Gore brain trust had run the campaign. James Carville had put up a famous sign in the Clinton–Gore war room reminding everybody, "It's the economy, stupid." I decided to be a copycat and had a huge banner made that covered a whole wall in our war room, screaming in twelve-inch high letters: "It's September 7th, stupid!"

That helped keep everybody's eyes on the objective. We needed a schedule that would help manage our progress toward the deadline. My engineering work and Pentagon experience made it easy. I decided to break up the remaining time—just under five months—into three equal parts: part one would be for "blue sky" work, in which we would look at a very wide range of proposals with little screening of really bad ideas. In part two, we would cull the best ideas from part one and refine them enough to present to the vice president for his decisions. In part three, we would write a report documenting the proposals he had approved at the end of part two.

It was easy to write out the schedule on paper, but I was in for a surprise, supplied by Gore.

"Oh, no you don't," he admonished me. "With your schedule, you get to make all the really interesting decisions. I want to be involved from the earliest stages, when the teams are just beginning to decide what issues to take on."

He started meeting with the teams—about twenty or thirty meetings, during which his concentration was total. He invited midlevel civil servants to speak their mind and even to argue with him. He always made the meetings fun. One of the first meetings ran into the evening. We were interrupted by his assistant, Beth Pritchard, who announced, "It's 6:30. You have to leave now. There are 2,000 people waiting for you at the Washington Hilton, and the color guard can't start until you get there."

"No I don't," he announced, stiffening his back and thrusting out his chest. "I'm the vice president."

Not to be intimidated, Pritchard shot back, "You think you're pretty cool, don't you!" He did. But he left a couple of minutes later when she returned, stamped her foot, and said, "Right now!"

Another time he told the team he was meeting with, "You're doing a *great* job. Keep it up . . . and try not to think of the terrible consequences of failure."

He liked poking fun at himself. He bounced into a meeting one morning and announced, "I saw [the film] *Dave* last night. You should all go see it. The vice president is the hero, and it's got a great ending—the president dies."

In another of the early meetings, Beverly Godwin, our budget team leader, brought in a three-foot stack of budget documents from her days at the Department of Health and Human Services. Godwin explained that they were just a tiny part of the forest-worth of totally useless documents that OMB required the department to assemble in the early stages of preparing the annual budget to be sent to Congress. Gore asked whether every department of government was required to do the same. When Godwin said they were, Gore explained, "I'm a believer in performance art. How about assembling a complete set of useless documents and piling them into a mound on the Plaza behind the Capitol? Then we'll get the cameras rolling, and I'll scale the hill in mountain climbing gear."

We never gave him the chance to scale the hill of useless documents, but we did find material to satisfy his desire for props.

In announcing the NPR, Clinton had invited Americans to participate by sending in any stories or evidence of government waste to "Al Gore, Reinventing Government, Washington, D.C." The mail started pouring in— baskets and baskets of it. We were overwhelmed and called for volunteers— people from a retirement home in the suburbs, college students, just about anybody.

One of the volunteers was sixteen-year-old David Kauvar, Gerry Kauvar's son. David had listened for years to his father's stories of government craziness, and he knew it when he saw it. He barged into my office clutching a sheaf of papers. "Look what I found," he proclaimed proudly.

It was a letter from the head of government sales at Libbey Glass Company explaining that if we wanted to reduce waste we might start with the way the government buys ashtrays. He enclosed a nine-page GSA specification, which read like a parody dreamed up by a comedian with a bizarre sense of humor.

To meet the government specifications and thus be eligible for purchase by the government, an ashtray—called in the specification an "ash receiver, tobacco (desk-type)"—must have the following characteristics:

> It must be square or round, and made of clear glass. If square, "it must have a minimum of four cigarette rests, spaced equidistant around the periphery and aimed at the center of the ash receiver, molded into the top. The cigarette rests shall be sloped toward the center of the ash receiver. The rests shall be parallel to the outside top edge of the receiver or in each corner, at the manufacturer's option. All surfaces shall be smooth."

There was also a requirement for testing the ashtray:

> The test shall be made by placing the specimen on its base upon a solid support (a 1-3/4 inch, 44.5 mm maple plank), placing a steel center punch (point ground to a 60-degree included angle) in contact with the center of the inside surface of the bottom and striking with a hammer in successive blows of increasing severity until breakage occurs. [When shattered] the specimen should break into a small number of irregular shaped pieces not greater in number than 35.

Not trusting the manufacturer to figure out what constitutes a "piece," it goes on to explain:

> Any piece 1/4 inch (6.4 mm) or more on any three of its adjacent edges (excluding the thickness dimension) shall be included in the number counted. Smaller fragments shall not be counted.[1]

I was overjoyed. I had discovered my calling at the Pentagon when I found examples of craziness that no sensible person could ignore—like the steam trap or the can of spray paint that had to be "revalidated" annually by the base chemist. These examples had helped me get the attention of top defense leadership and such outsiders as Tom Peters and David Osborne—not to mention Al Gore—and mobilize their support for reform.

I now had a wonderful piece of government craziness that Gore could own. I called the Libbey executive and asked him to FedEx me a couple of ash receivers, desk type. Next morning I fairly ran to Gore's office with an ash receiver, desk type, and specification in hand. He was as excited as I, and as luck would have it, he had an interview that day with Joe Klein of *Newsweek*.

When Klein arrived Gore told him, "Listen to this," and read him the first couple pages of the specification. A few days later, I opened my August 16, 1993, copy of *Newsweek* to see a full-page column by Klein about the vice president's ashtray, explaining to millions of readers how government rules and regulations had gotten out of control and needed to be reinvented.

Gore always urged his staff to be bold and to consider radical changes. One day, for reasons I've forgotten, he jumped on me. "You're thinking too narrowly. You're not being bold enough or looking at a wide enough range of options."

I was prepared for this, or so I thought.

"We're looking at every single dollar the government spends except for interest on the debt," I shot back.

Gore was unfazed. "Why aren't you looking at that?'

"Because there's nothing we could do about it if we wanted to."[2]

"Why not?" he fired back. He paused to think for just about three seconds. "We could announce we're not paying it this year." Long pause ... "Just kidding."

In addition to urging us to be bold, he told us not to worry about politics while we did our analysis. He was soon challenged on this point when one of the teams briefed him on their intention to propose that the government sell the Tennessee Valley Authority (TVA). The staff waited breathlessly for his reaction.

"Well, as a congressman and as a senator, I've always supported TVA because I thought it was the right thing to do. But if you can show me that there is a solid benefit to selling it off, I'll reconsider."

That story got around NPR and was taken by the staff as evidence that he was really serious about reinventing government and wanted us not to rule anything out.

The team did try to make a case for selling TVA, but could never make a very convincing one. In a similar vein, another team told him it wanted to significantly cut the number of political appointees. The proposal wouldn't be very popular in the White House, where there was a frenzy to fill every one of those jobs. Still, Gore encouraged them to develop the issue, but they never could make a persuasive case.

Gore believed in listening to everybody. When NPR was formed, he insisted that every member of the NPR staff—about 200 career civil servants—be connected to him by e-mail. He usually answered my e-mails the same day, often within a minute or two.

The staff members weren't always politically savvy about e-mails they sent to Gore. Once a series of subpoenaed e-mails appeared on the front page of the *Los Angeles Times* and other newspapers. The e-mails were very colorful and very controversial. Doug Farbrother, the career civil servant who sent them, felt terrible about embarrassing the boss. Several days later, Doug sent Gore a midnight e-mail congratulating the vice president on his debate with Ross Perot. Gore responded before dawn.

"Thanks. Oh, by the way, I want you to know how pleased I am about all the headlines. They will make it clear to our friends how hard we're working for them."

After that experience, Doug was ready to march into fire for a boss who would stand by you even after you got him into hot water.

As bold as Gore wanted us to be, the OMB tried to impose timidity on us. OMB's career staff had an organizational resentment toward NPR, who they regarded (with some accuracy) as amateurs who had usurped OMB's rightful role as custodians of government management.

I was as annoyed with OMB as they were with me—so much so that my good manners left me one day in a large meeting that included Gore and Alice Rivlin, OMB's number two. Rivlin was brilliant and as nice a person as ever occupied a high position in government. She was arguing for a larger role in reinvention for OMB.

I snapped at her. "Our job is to reinvent the government. You *are* the government."

Rivlin took this with good nature, even when Gore burst out laughing. I proceeded to show them a briefing about our proposal to cut government employment by 252,000. Most outsiders thought that the cut was the work of politicos who wanted something with public relations punch, but it really was the work of three career DOD executives—Doug Farbrother, Duncan Holaday, and me. We had cut our management teeth on the DOD MIP and knew firsthand how debilitating to morale and quality was the huge number of overseers at headquarters.

Our passion was fueled by the analysis of one of the NPR teams, showing that *one federal employee in three* was either in headquarters or performing a control function—supervisors, IGs, comptrollers, auditors, or procurement and personnel clerks whose job was mainly to manage, control, check up on, or audit others. We remembered General Creech's warning, "There's a war on between the people who are trying to do something and the people who are trying to keep them from doing something wrong."

We were solidly on the side of the doers. On a briefing slide, I labeled the target—the headquarters and control types—"forces of central control and mistrust."

When Gore saw the label, he complained. "That's a bad term. People won't know who you're talking about."

I couldn't resist another jab at OMB.

"To make it widely understandable, we're proposing to change the name of OMB to the Office of Central Control and Mistrust."

Nobody in the room thought that was funny—not Rivlin, not even Gore.

Gore was delighted, however, with the proposed cut. He asked what percent of the total employment we wanted to cut. We said, "Twelve percent." Phil Lader suggested, "Why not ten percent?" to which Gore replied, "Why not twelve?" Twelve it was. This one action would by itself redeem our pledge to make government cost less, saving $40 billion over five years.

The cuts had mixed results. The money saved delivered one of NPR's twin goals: to make government work better and cost less. But all our talk about the cuts made many top civil servants—the very people who would have to deliver the "works better" goal—cynical about NPR, considering it merely *this* administration's technique for cutting federal jobs. Matters worsened when Gore accepted Phil Lader's offer for OMB to administer the cuts. OMB merely slapped on fierce head count controls, which were anathema to reinventors; the cuts in the forces of "central control and mistrust" were largely forgotten, except at GSA and the Office of Personnel Management (OPM), where the directors themselves believed in streamlining management.

From my first day with Gore, I burned with an uncontrollable desire to get him to Langley Air Force Base, the home of TAC (now called Air Combat

Command, or ACC), where "pilots in red scarves flew airplanes with red tails maintained by mechanics in red caps." That's where I had learned the power of decentralization and deregulation, and I wanted the boss to learn what I had learned firsthand from the four-star general. General Bill Creech had retired nine years earlier, but the current commander, General Mike Loh, was a disciple of Creech's and a fanatic about the Creech style of leadership.

The demands on the vice president's time were intense, and his travel schedule was driven more by politics than by reinvention. I made a pest of myself around his office, and I never stopped needling Elaine Kamarck about getting Gore to Langley. I even offered to introduce her to glamorous Brigadier General "Boomer" McBroom, the fighter wing commander who had become something of a sex symbol during his telecasts from Saudi Arabia before and during the Gulf War in 1991.

Finally, Elaine delivered. Gore would stop at Langley on a multiday trip that would take him all over the country. I called Mike Loh to brief him about what to show Gore, but he needed no advice from me. He was a natural.

He greeted Gore at the steps to Air Force Two and presented him with a leather flight jacket, which Gore put on. He looked great in it, but his political staff insisted he take it off lest he remind people of Michael Dukakis, whose presidential campaign was ridiculed after he allowed himself to be photographed looking very dorky as he drove an Army tank in full battle regalia.

The Langley visit was wonderful. After the greeting, Loh gave Gore a long briefing that laid out the ACC approach to leadership, along with numbers proving its superiority to the traditional command-and-control Soviet style system popularized by Frederick Taylor and his spiritual heir, Robert McNamara. I was afraid Gore was going to be irritated by the long briefing, but he was really captured by it.

Loh took Gore through the hangars and shops where he met airmen of all ranks and occupations who were bursting with pride as they told the vice president of the United States about how they were saving millions of dollars while operating the most powerful, readiest military force in the world.

Loh had built on Creech's fanatical decentralization and deregulation. ACC aircraft mechanics had been prohibited from repairing many broken aircraft parts—instead they removed the part, shipped it to the repair depot in Utah, and replaced it with a new part or one that had been rebuilt at the depot. Loh let mechanics repair parts that they had been trained on. One example: it cost just $300 to have ACC mechanics replace old seals in the F15 hydraulic reservoirs, compared to a $13,000 repair at the depot. Savings to the taxpayers: $12,700 per F15, of which the Air Force owned 1,300. Loh kept a running total of the savings, which ran close to $100 million in 1993 alone.

Gore listened to the briefing and to the airmen's stories with the total concentration of which he was capable and carried away the conviction that the TAC approach—decentralization, deregulation of the front lines, and catering to the human spirit—was *the* way to operate. He started to use TAC examples in his speeches and called on Mike Loh several times for advice and help in teaching reinvention.

Gore and Kamarck decided to continue his education—and teaching—by holding a reinventing government summit meeting, which would bring together top experts in leadership and management from corporate America, academia, and governments of all sorts—federal, state, city, and foreign. He insisted on having Mike Loh as the last speaker, because he wanted to punctuate the day with an example of government working extraordinarily well.

Gore chose to hold the summit in Congress Hall in Philadelphia, where the first Continental Congress had voted to adopt the Declaration of Independence. To Gore, the symbolism was perfect. He saw reinvention as crucial to restoring Americans' trust in government, which in turn was crucial to, in his words, "redeeming the promise of Philadelphia."

He listened and taught well that day. From Joseph Juran, the ninety-year-old patron saint of quality management, he heard to trust the worker. From Frank Doyle, the executive vice president of General Electric, he heard to move boldly and quickly. Doyle said, apropos of his GE experience, "We could always have been faster. We did not set goals high enough; we did not move quickly enough."

The academics urged Gore to be cautious lest he make a mistake. I always thought their subliminal message was that he could avoid mistakes if he hired academics.

Gore didn't listen to the voices of caution. Many times over the next few years, he rejected calls to bring in experts to tell him how to reform government, insisting that he already had the real experts—the people who worked there. Hooray.

I took Doyle's advice to heart. Every change we were considering had a down side—if only we gave the opposition enough time to marshal its arguments and its forces. I had learned the perils of moving too slowly at the Pentagon, where our attempts to close unneeded military bases had been stymied for years by a sensible-sounding law—the National Environmental Policy Act (NEPA)—that required the government to move slowly and to carefully consider the impact of its actions on the environment.

The trouble was that while we were considering all the alternatives, each one with its own possible impacts, we were developing ammunition for adversaries to use to stop us. For example, when the Pentagon announced that it was considering closing Fort Dix, New Jersey, and moving training that was being done there to Fort Jackson, South Carolina, and to Fort Leonard Wood, Missouri, we were required by NEPA to consider the alternative of moving training *into* Fort Dix from the other bases. And while we were considering all the alternatives, some reasonable, some not, none having any substantial environmental impact, opponents of the closing—typically local business interests supported by their congressional delegations—brought all their guns to bear on the poor Pentagon. Result: *no* bases were closed for more than ten years, until the law was changed.

The White House was no different. Every bit of pork barrel spending had its defenders who could explain that it was not pork at all but good public policy. Every time the reinvention team proposed a cut, the defenders would come out of the woodwork to fight us. For example, when we proposed to hold farm subsidies to a maximum of $100,000 per farmer, Senator Dale Bumpers learned of it and called his old Arkansas friend, President Clinton, and explained that many farmers who were getting huge subsidies employed poor Arkansan sharecroppers who would be thrown out of work if the subsidies were capped. That was the end of our attempt to cap farm subsidies.

One way to defeat the defenders of the status quo was to move fast before they could mobilize their allies. Another way was to keep our plans secret so they would be taken by surprise when we unveiled our proposals. And if our proposals had some bitter medicine for *all* interest groups, opponents of any particular change could be made to look selfish when they opposed it. Of course, sometimes the defenders of the status quo had facts we didn't have that could have helped us avoid mistakes, but that was a risk we were willing to take. The biggest mistake for now was timidity.

Another reason for secrecy was to build up interest and suspense. We believed, correctly, that the press would cover a big splash by NPR, but that press interest would be greatly diminished if the news were allowed to dribble out.

The White House leaked copiously, but Elaine Kamarck and the vice president were fanatical about preserving the big news: total dollars saved and jobs cut. When we were getting ready to brief the president, Elaine ordered me to prepare copies of the presentation only for the people who would be in the Oval Office briefing: one each for the president, David Gergen, George Stephanopoulos, the vice president, her, and me.

We numbered each copy, but that turned out to be unnecessary. At the end of the meeting, the vice president retrieved every copy from the attendees, including the president's copy.

"I'm guarding against leaks," he told the president.

"Good judgment," the president laughed, as he handed over his copy.

Leaks had a variety of causes, sometimes malice, sometimes someone just being a blabbermouth. I was the inadvertent source of one leak, simply because I was outsmarted.

Two days before our report was to be released, I got a call from a producer at *ABC News*. ABC was planning wide coverage of our report, and the producer made a reasonable sounding request.

"I know you can't divulge your recommendations to the president," she started, sweetly, "but you could still help us with our coverage. We're sending crews out to government locations that are likely to be affected, and maybe you could save us from wasting a lot of money by sending crews where there won't be any news."

"Sorry," I answered, "but I can't tell you anything."

"You don't have to," she assured me. "I'll read off a list of places we're planning to send crews to, and you just listen and don't say anything unless you think we're making a mistake."

That sounded innocuous enough. Her list included only places that would be affected by our recommendations, so I said nothing. She thanked me.

Ten minutes later my phone rang. It was Marla Romash, the vice president's communications director. Marla was extraordinarily territorial about the media—all contacts went through her, and heaven help the person who violated the rule.

"BOB STONE, *ABC NEWS* SAYS YOU JUST CONFIRMED THAT WE'RE GOING TO MOVE THE FOOD SAFETY INSPECTION SERVICE FROM AGRICULTURE TO THE FDA. IS THAT TRUE?" she demanded.

"Well, yes, I guess it is," I admitted, fearfully. But Marla had a soft spot for me and let me off with a mild admonition about being more careful next time.

In mid-August, we were ready to take our recommendations to the president. I put together a presentation of about fifty charts, and Gore briefed the president. He and Clinton had a remarkable meeting of the minds on just about every issue. We were fixing the things that had driven Clinton nuts when he was governor, and he really liked the package, except for a relative handful of recommendations that he considered political poison. I already mentioned our proposal to limit subsidies to rich farmers. We also proposed abolishing the Selective Service System (the United States hasn't drafted anybody since 1974 and is unlikely ever to do so again), which the president vetoed, along with a few others.

For the most part, Clinton nodded, smiled, and interrupted with sounds of approval and enthusiasm. The meeting went very smoothly, although it was interrupted for an urgent military matter.

Dee Dee Myers, Clinton's press secretary, tiptoed into the Oval Office when we were halfway through and whispered something to David Gergen.

"Mr. President," Gergen interjected, "Did you know General Mundy [the Commandant of the Marine Corps] was going to bar enlistment to married people?"

Clinton slapped his hand to his head and slowly slid out of his chair onto the floor.

"Great! Who says we don't have a family policy for the military? We take gays, we just don't take married people."

General Mundy rescinded his order the next day, but the episode, while good for a laugh, didn't help Clinton's relations with the military brass.

When the meeting broke up, around 10 P.M., we had the president's approval on a package of about 1,200 recommendations. Many of them would have a huge effect on government, like streamlining procurement, reforming the civil service system, converting the Federal Aviation Administration's (FAA) air traffic control system to a government corporation with directors representing the airlines, cutting the number of overseers and checkers in government, forming a President's Management Council, and integrating Customs and Immigration staffs at border crossings and international airports. The list went on and on.

Many of our recommendations were transformational, most were sensible, and a few were mistakes. All together, though, they made up a stack of mind-numbing papers that nobody would read. We needed somehow to turn them into a report that students of government and reporters would read and comprehend.

The task seemed impossible to me, but David Osborne knew just what to do. He assembled an extraordinary team of talented writers who understood the substance of what we were proposing: Kate Sylvester, Larry Haas, Roger Vaughan, and Janet Topolsky. The team was brilliant, willing to work all night, and full of wicked humor. Janet wanted us to adopt as a goal-making government procurement as simple as buying a handgun. Sounded good to me, but cooler heads prevailed.

Within a month, David and his team had produced a page-turner of a report. We no longer just had a pile of 1,200 recommendations; we had a real book that would be fun to read. All that remained was to run it by the White House staff. We gave them just a couple of days to review the book and let us know if it contained any egregious mistakes. We got tons of suggested changes from at least thirty-five people, including Gore's chief of staff. Many of the changes would have torn the heart out of the report. Elaine Kamarck made it clear that David was in charge, and David ignored most of them.

We had not yet heard from OMB. I dreaded what they might say, so I wasn't unhappy when they missed my deadline for commenting. Just as I was ready to take the manuscript to the printer, I looked out the window and, to my dismay, saw Bill Halter, assistant to OMB deputy Phil Lader, crossing 17th Street with a pile of papers under his arm. The feared OMB comments were coming after all.

I panicked. I waited at the back door of the NPR suite until I heard the elevator doors open. I gave Halter just enough time to get in the front door, then I slipped out the back door, into the elevator, and out into the night. I had outsmarted OMB. Their changes were too late. The book was at the printer.

Alas, I had not outsmarted Halter. He called Elaine at home, and she told him where the printer was and to take his comments to me there. Then they negotiated by phone the few changes we would make. The changes made the report just a little worse, and nobody but me would ever notice.

We had a bestseller, a book that Max Depree, former CEO and author of popular business books, called "the best book on management available in America." Plume Books and Times Books both decided to print it commercially as *Creating a Government that Works Better and Costs Less.*

Plume Books got Tom Peters to write an enthusiastic foreword and the book made the *New York Times* bestseller list. *Time* called it "the most readable federal document in memory."

September 7 in Washington was bright and clear. Doug Farbrother, our impresario, had set the stage. Behind the president's podium, four-by-four-foot pallets lay everywhere, stacked with government reports of all sizes, shapes, and colors—paperback reports, handsomely bound books of laws and regulations, and huge three-ring binders. Pallets of documents rested atop other pallets of documents. Behind the pallets, the two biggest forklifts I had ever seen were stacked about ten feet high with government rules and regulations we'd recommended for elimination, all neatly bound in red tape for the occasion.

The South Lawn of the White House was lined with television cameras and several hundred chairs. Everybody was there—the Cabinet, the subcabinet, Washington opinion makers, press from around the world, and, of course, the NPR staff—250 strong.

Gore told the president, "This report will tell us how to cut waste, cut red tape, streamline the bureaucracy, change procurement rules, change the personnel rules, and create a government that works better and costs less."

The president raised everybody's spirits with his response: "There are lots of places in this report where it says 'the president should,' 'the president should.' Well, let me tell you something, I've read it, and where it says 'the president should,' this president will." That night, reinventing government led all the network newscasts, and it made the front page—above the fold—in every major newspaper and most minor ones.

We had done it! We had created a blueprint for making government work better and cost less, we had earned a smashing presidential endorsement, and we had done it on time and without any of the screwups that had plagued Clinton's first year—the health care fiasco, travelgate, gays in the military.

Our book was on the bestseller list. It was just about time to take in all the praise and rest on our laurels. Or so I thought.

LESSONS FROM CHAPTER EIGHT: GETTING A BIG JOB DONE IN A HURRY

—Set impossible deadlines, keep everyone focused on them, and meet them, whatever it takes.

—Set impossible goals and work like crazy to meet them.

—Put your goals and principles on a wallet-size card and circulate the cards promiscuously.

—Keep people informed: hold frequent staff meetings; if your team is spread out appoint a town crier.

—Get top leadership involved early—that's when the key decisions really get made.

—Side with the people who are trying to *do* something, not with the people who are trying to keep them from doing something wrong.

—To create change, move fast.

NOTES

1. General Services Administration Regulation AA-A-710E (superseding Regulation AA-A-710D).

2. I was wrong about this. Shortly, with no help from NPR, the Treasury did reduce interest costs by issuing short-term notes to pay off long-term bonds that had come due. Since short-term rates were substantially lower than long-term rates, Treasury lowered interest costs by billions.

Setting a Thousand Fires and Fanning the Flames

(Encouraging and Protecting Innovators)

The White House message machine decided to publicize NPR in a big way—the president and vice president would tour the country doing events to attract media attention to reinventing government, or ReGo, as it was known around the White House. My reward was to get to go on the trip with no responsibilities. It was the kind of boondoggle I was usually too puritanical to go on, but it seemed like another once-in-a-lifetime opportunity, and Elaine Kamarck urged me to go, after strong-arming the White House for an invitation for me.

The vice president and his party, including me, were to take off from Andrews Air Force Base on Air Force Two,[1] headed for Cleveland, Ohio, where the first ReGo event was to be held: the president would sign a Presidential Memorandum establishing the President's Community Enterprise Board to help communities solve their problems with customer-friendly support from the federal government.

Soon after Air Force Two was airborne, the president would take off in Air Force One. That way the vice president would be on the tarmac with the mayor of Cleveland to welcome the president when he landed. My assignment from Elaine was to relax, have fun, and bask in the glory of a job well done. I should have known better.

We were a few minutes out from Cleveland when I was summoned to the vice president's compartment.

"The president just called and asked where are all the executive orders we promised to get him to sign."

I should have been looking forward to this question, but I had been dreading it. NPR had made dozens of recommendations for presidential actions, many of them executive orders, but we were getting nowhere in the White House bureaucracy. For example, the White House Counsel's office thought it was silly to issue an executive order on customer service, never mind that the president had decided to do it.

"The White House lawyers have us tied up in knots," I replied, weakly. "They don't like our ideas. [In fact, they were now objecting not to NPR ideas but to the presidential decisions they had become.] We're not getting anywhere on the executive orders we need."

Gore was painfully clear. "I want at least three executive orders to hand the president to sign by the time we land at Moffitt Field tonight." (Moffitt Field was a Naval air station in California's Silicon Valley, our next stop after Cleveland.)

There went my carefree boondoggle. At Cleveland I found a desk and a phone in the airport offices and spent all our ground time on the phone with Elaine, figuring out which orders to go for and how to get them done.

Elaine was an irresistible force. That night we had three new orders for the president: streamlining the bureaucracy, setting standards for customer service, and eliminating half of the executive branch's internal regulations.

Haste sometimes gets it wrong, though. The staff member who drafted the order on streamlining had gotten one number right (a cut of 252,000 federal employees) and one wrong. We had decided to cut the ratio of supervisors-and-managers to other employees in half, but the draft of the presidential memo called for the ratio to be doubled. We called back to Washington around midnight, California time—3 A.M. in D.C.—and got the staffer out of bed and back to the White House to make one simple change: for "double" substitute "halve." He made the change and faxed it back to the Sunnyvale hotel, where the fax machine printed out a yellowish copy on thermal paper for the president to sign.

From then on, the trip was a blast for me, riding in presidential motorcades, attending a dinner given in the vice president's honor by the big names of Silicon Valley, passing through Secret Service security lines.

Sunnyvale is a midsize California city that had been far ahead of everybody in making government customer friendly and entrepreneurial. NPR often used Sunnyvale as the model of reinvention. I enjoyed needling OMB people by saying that I wanted to make the United States government just like Sunnyvale's. This alarmed the OMBers, who rushed to restate the obvious: governing a city of 120,000 was very different from governing a nation of 250 million.

At NPR, we had talked so much about Sunnyvale and put it into so many of the president's and vice president's speeches that the Sunnyvale paper ran a front page cartoon the day of our visit showing Clinton proclaiming to a rally, *"Ich bin ein* Sunnyvaler."

The trip had been planned to last a week, but Clinton cut it short after a stop in Houston to push the North American Free Trade Agreement. He needed to return to host Yasser Arafat and Yitzhak Rabin at the White House. The famous handshake swept NPR off the news pages. It was time to get back to work.

That was all right with me. I was anxious to get started on reinvention. We had spent six months putting together a plan for what we were *going* to do. I had had enough of planning and was ready to start doing.

Like most people, I wanted to see results fast. In the spring of 1993, literally before we knew what we were doing at NPR, I had gotten Gore to sign a letter encouraging agency heads to designate some of their activities as "reinvention laboratories." Back in defense, the model installations had quickly identified bureaucratic craziness and inefficiencies, and helped make an overwhelming case for decentralization and deregulation. Reinvention labs were model installations with a different name; they would do the same for the government as a whole.

Nothing that you could put your finger on was really changed for the reinvention labs. No laws were changed; no new organizations were established. Agency heads were simply encouraged to delegate some of their authority to the "labs" and to respond quickly and positively to their requests for waivers of rules. The entrepreneurial-minded quickly rushed to take advantage of the promised freedom.

Within a few weeks, we had our first success. The Gulfport, Mississippi, office of the Department of Agriculture's Animal and Plant Health Inspection Service (the people who keep plant pests and animal diseases from entering the country) had been designated a reinvention lab. One night the office was burglarized, and its two laptop computers were stolen. Since the Gulfport inspectors used the laptops to record their inspections, they were faced with something of an emergency.

Jerry Bolden, the office head, called the procurement office in Minneapolis (!) and asked for replacements to be delivered lickety-split.

"C'mon," the procurement officer told him. "You know the rules. Put in a requisition, and you'll get them when you get them." Past experience said that would likely take months, at the least, so Bolden, encouraged by the Gulfport office's status as a reinvention lab, went to the local computer store, charged two laptops, and sent the bill to Minneapolis after stamping it with a rubber stamp he had made: "PURCHASED IN ACCORDANCE WITH AL GORE'S PRINCIPLES OF REINVENTING GOVERNMENT."

We found out about it and immediately told Gore and got him to congratulate Secretary of Agriculture Mike Espy on the entrepreneurial spirit Espy had unleashed. Soon we had a hero of reinvention that we could tell federal employees about, urging them to show his spirit. I told the story in every speech and every briefing I gave on ReGo.

Several years later, I visited Minneapolis and hesitated to repeat the story at the office that was the butt of the joke, because I was uncertain that it had happened exactly that way. So I asked the head of the Minneapolis office. "Yes it did," he told me. "People here tried to get Bolden fired, but we could hardly fire him after Gore made a hero of him."

We read about another early success in the paper. Don Kettl, a professor at the University of Wisconsin, wrote an article assessing reinvention. Instead of just reading our White House press releases or talking to other academics, he visited the Veterans Hospital in Milwaukee, which had been designated a reinvention lab; he found it a hotbed of change. He wrote that reinvention was indeed real.[2]

Now we had to deliver on our plan. When the report was done, most of the staff of 250 went back to the agencies we had borrowed them from, but about forty-five of us stayed on—to wrap things up, I thought, although it turned out that wrapping things up took seven years, not the few months we had expected. After Clinton's intervention, we did pretty well on presidential directives, getting twelve signed in less than a month and five more in the next month. We also had to finish more than thirty supplementary reports detailing our recommendations and their rationale.

Pretty soon three months had gone by since our report to the president. Somebody suggested we have a reunion for the NPR "alumni" who had returned to their parent agencies. It turned out to be a dreary affair, much more

so because the attendees had been to the mountaintop and now were back below sea level. I found it depressing and the next day mentioned it to Gore.

"What did you learn?" he asked.

"Lots of stuff," I replied. "One person told his boss about serving customers, and his boss snapped back, 'We don't have customers, we have suspects.' Another started preaching empowerment, and her boss said, 'If you
empower your subordinates, then what do I need you for?' And when a third
suggested getting rid of some red tape, her boss told her that it wasn't red
tape, it was POLICY."

"I guess I learned that people in government don't get our lingo—they
don't know what we're talking about when we say put customers first, empower employees, and cut red tape," I replied.

"Then I'll have to teach them," Gore said. "I want to visit every department
and independent agency to personally teach them the principles of reinvention."

I recalled my experience at the Pentagon when I had attended a two-day
offsite held by the Undersecretary of Defense, John Betti, to teach 200 defense
executives how to introduce quality management into our work. This was
three years after my introduction of quality management (I called it "Excellent
Installations"), but I still learned a lot and got new inspiration from the speakers and the workshops.

One of the speakers was Ralph Stayer, CEO of Johnsonville Sausage, who
told the gathering of defense executives how he had increased feelings of ownership in his employees when he gave up his prerogative of tasting the product to see if it was good enough to ship and delegated that final quality check
to the production team.

Stayer was the last speaker before lunch, and I was high from listening to
him. I joined seven of my colleagues at a table for lunch and bubbled, "What
did you all think of the last speaker?"

"Sausage!!" One of them curled his lip with disdain. "What do sausages
have to do with defense!" "Yeah, sausage!" another said. "What were they
thinking about when they invited that guy?" Nobody at the table except me
thought there was any significance for DOD in Stayer's experience that employees who were given real responsibility became more committed to the enterprise.

The sausage experience showed me that most defense people wouldn't
learn from examples of reinvention at a sausage factory; they needed to have

examples from defense. Similarly, the best way to teach reinvention to people in the Department of Veterans Affairs was to show them veteran affairs examples. And so on. So we went to work looking for examples that would serve as heroes of reinvention.

The first one we found was Joe Thompson, head of the Veterans Affairs (VA) benefits office in New York City. Joe is a laconic New Yorker, a Vietnam veteran with a passion to follow Lincoln's aim "to care for him who shall have borne the battle, and for his widow and orphan." Joe had taken an old-line bureaucracy and transformed it. To teach workers about veterans, Joe took them to veterans' hospitals where they spent time getting to know their customers. To relieve the mind-numbing monotony of most of the jobs, he formed the workers into teams that collaborated on dealing with the totality of a veteran's claim instead of having one person to record the claim, one to check for completeness of medical records, one to search for military service records, and so on. To allow veterans to check on the status of their claims, he formed all employees into teams, assigned every claim to a team, and routed each vet's telephone calls to the team that was handling his claim. And to give workers and bosses a scorecard, he measured timeliness and accuracy of claim resolution, customer satisfaction, employee satisfaction, and cost per claim. In short, Joe changed everything and measured the results.

The results were astounding. The New York office had a waiting room that had regularly been packed with vets waiting to file a claim or to find out the status of a claim they had filed long ago. The new processes sped things up so much that the waiting room was no longer needed. Joe converted it into a museum of veterans history. Now veterans were satisfied and workers who had been on the verge of being disciplined for bad performance became enthusiastic and productive. We had our first hero. We'd bring Joe to Washington to VA headquarters, where Gore would spotlight his team as the example of reinvention.

Joe, like any civil servant who was creating change, was not all that popular with headquarters, which—like most headquarters—was quite satisfied with the status quo. They were skeptical about honoring Joe. When I told them about how Joe had ended the waiting lines in New York, one headquarters staffer scoffed. "Vets like to stand in line. It gives them a chance to meet other vets and swap war stories."[3]

Joe didn't want a fuss made over him. When I told him what I had in mind, he told me he didn't want those people in Washington to know what he was doing.

But Joe Thompson's story was too perfect an example of reinvention to pass up. Gore decided to bring Joe to Washington and gave him an award in front of the VA secretary and brass.

The first day I met Gore, he had talked about awards. He recalled that former Senator William Proxmire had received a great deal of publicity for his "Golden Fleece" (as in "fleece the taxpayer") awards given to, or rather hung on, some government worker or organization that had done something wasteful of government money. Gore wanted to give an award for excellence, for doing something worthy of honor rather than scorn. He mulled names over on his tongue. The only one I remember was a "silver floss" award. We hadn't done anything with Gore's idea, but now it was time to resurrect it.

I don't remember who came up with the idea of a hammer award, but Gore loved it. We got an ordinary hardware store six-dollar hammer, tied twenty cents worth of red, white, and blue ribbon in a bow around the handle, mounted it on a velvet-covered board with a handwritten card signed by Al Gore, and enclosed it in a gold-anodized aluminum frame. Gore played it against the Pentagon's mythical $400 hammer, saying the old government had a $400 hammer, but we were presenting a six-dollar hammer. He occasionally broke into song, "If I had a hammer . . ."

Including labor, the hammer award probably cost $100. Best of all, we found a company that sold hammer-shaped lapel pins for forty-four cents. We could afford to give the big, framed award to the team leader and give a lapel pin to every member of the team we were honoring. The lapel pins were highly prized and worn with pride.

Eventually we would give out 1,378 hammer awards and 68,000 lapel pins to teams that did something extraordinary to further the principles of reinventing government. We were never able, of course, to total up their achievements, but the nominations for the awards, which were vetted and approved by parent agencies, claimed savings of more than $53 billion. Perhaps best of all for reinvention, we had left a mark—or at least a lapel pin—on 68,000 people.

We used the awards strategically, always honoring behavior we wanted people to emulate and sometimes stepping in to put Gore's imprimatur on reinventors who were under some kind of threat.

For example, some Food and Drug Administration (FDA) inspectors in California had figured out that they could better advance public health and safety if they helped small biotech companies prepare for an FDA inspection, rather than stay aloof and play "gotcha" at inspection time. They considered themselves partners to the industry, rather than adversaries, and this was threatening to the traditionalists at headquarters.

Marie Urban, leader of reinvention in FDA's office of regulatory affairs, was definitely *not* a traditionalist. She had long since figured out that FDA's job was to further public health, not mindlessly to act as an adversary of the industries that produced food, medicines, and medical devices. She called NPR in a panic; FDA lawyers were preparing a new policy directive that would enshrine adversarial behavior and rule out the budding practice of FDA acting as a "partner" to industry—the "p-word," they called it.

The lawyers never knew what hit them. I traveled to San Diego to give the California biotech inspectors a hammer award, Gore congratulated Secretary of Health and Human Services Donna Shalala, and I gave an interview to *Inside FDA*, a trade publication that everybody in the business reads, about FDA's great step forward in public health through partnership and how Gore had honored them with his prestigious award. The policy directive disappeared, and partnership became an acceptable concept.

The hammer awards played a central role in what I described as our arson strategy: set 1,000 fires and fan the flames. Marie Urban and her colleagues at FDA had set a fire of reinvention. With the hammer award, we were fanning the flames. Soon Marie was meeting with reinventors from other regulatory agencies to teach them about partnership. The fires of reinvention were spreading, and the lawyers couldn't stamp them out.

When we dragged Joe Thompson to Washington to get the first hammer award, I had no idea where it would lead. Since telling me he didn't want to come to D.C. and he didn't want the people at headquarters to know what he was doing in New York, Joe had managed to break his leg playing basketball. Now he told me he *couldn't* come to Washington. Since he was going to work every day, albeit on crutches, I ignored his protest.

We sent out film director *extraordinaire* Patrick Davidson to the New York VA office to get some videotape of the new operation. Davidson is a gifted television artist who had been under retainer to the Disney Channel. John Cooke, Disney president and a heavyweight in democratic politics, lent us Davidson to produce training videos. Davidson described his presence with us as "courtesy of the Mouse" (Mickey, that is).

It's illegal for the vice president's office to accept gifts, so we attempted to get OPM, which was allowed to accept gifts, to accept Davidson's services on NPR's behalf. But OPM was a creature of the unreinvented government. They procrastinated and threw up delay tactics. All the while, Davidson was filming. Finally they told us it was too late; we had accepted his services and they wouldn't create retroactive paperwork to cover the illegal gift we had already accepted. So we gave him a contract for one dollar to make videos for us. That satisfied the lawyers.

Davidson filmed VA workers speaking with passion about how the new process had changed their work life from deadening bureaucracy where they performed rote tasks to an uplifting mission where they looked veterans in the eye and helped "these American heroes," one worker said, "get the benefits they earned." One woman spoke of the pleasure she got from greeting the veterans and making them laugh. A representative of the Disabled American Veterans, a perennial adversary of VA over poor service, told the camera how well served and satisfied her customers were with the new office.

Davidson's video was powerful. It made us laugh and cry and swell with pride in federal service. It was even more powerful when introduced by Al Gore, seated on a barstool next to Joe Thompson—precarious on his crutches—and the people who were in the video, to an audience of the VA secretary and hundreds of VA executives and workers in the VA auditorium. It was the first hammer award the vice president made and the first of his forays into teaching federal workers about reinvention. He was to repeat the performance in every department and major agency, using Davidson's videos of workers from that department doing extraordinary things to serve customers, empower employees, or cut red tape.

(Joe had a point with his aversion to publicity, though. Within days, Congress commissioned an inquiry by the dreaded GAO into the claims Joe had made of improved morale and customer satisfaction. While no government executive ever wants to see the GAO, in this case the GAO validated all the claimed improvements.)

Gore loved his role as teacher and was very good at it. In March 1994, he was invited by Georgetown University to give the first speech in a series the university was kicking off to honor Marver Bernstein, a popular professor of political science who had recently died. The subject was to be "the new job of the federal executive." What could better serve the needs of reinvention!

The job of writing the speech fell to NPR's John Kamensky and Bob Lehrman, Gore's lead speechwriter. After struggling through a first draft, they were sent back to the drawing board by Gore. They did a new draft that started, as any good speech should, with an anecdote about the honoree, Marver Bernstein. I went with them to an early morning meeting with Gore to review the speech.

Gore had slept little the night before and was in an uncommonly grouchy mood.

"I don't like it," Gore opened the meeting. "I don't even like the anecdote about Bernstein. Don't you have another one?" he asked Lehrman.

"I only know one other anecdote," Lehrman replied. "Marver Bernstein and his wife saved up and went to Egypt on vacation. The hotel they were staying at burned down, and they both were killed."

"All right," Gore grumbled reluctantly. "Use the first one." He didn't like the substance of the speech and sent the team away to redo it.

Time was running out, and Kamensky and I were searching our brains for a formula that would do justice to reinvention and to Gore. Suddenly I remembered a speech I had used many times when I had been preaching reform at the Pentagon. I called it the "Entrepreneurial Leader," and it had a simple structure and message that contrasted old and new.

The old, which I labeled "contra-preneurial leadership," defends the status quo, avoids risk, centralizes decision making, and fixes unexpected failures. The new entrepreneurial leadership does just the reverse. It welcomes change, encourages sensible risk taking, decentralizes decision making, and builds on unexpected successes.

That was all Kamensky needed. Inspired, he dashed off a brilliant draft that took the entrepreneurial leader idea to a new level with theory and history, starting with Frederick Taylor, the father of the old idea that there was one right way to do any job. He and Lehrman showed it to Gore, and Gore liked it enough to build on it, revise it, add his flourishes about the parallels between modern leadership theory and massively parallel computing, and keep rewriting it until thirty minutes *after* the announced time for the speech.

The speech was a big hit. We had it recorded and printed as a booklet, "The New Job of the Federal Executive," which we handed out by the thousands to educate federal executives about Gore's and our hopes and expectations for them.

Through everything that was happening, Gore kept his commitment to reinvention. After the Republicans won both houses of Congress in 1994, Gore announced to us one day, "Guess who called me! Newt [Gingrich, then-speaker of the house]! He wants me to brief the Republican caucus on reinvention."

Of course Gore had accepted with relish. It caused consternation around the White House, Gore told us later, because how could he brief the Republican caucus when he hadn't briefed the Democrats? "Because they haven't invited me," he explained.

It was arranged that Gore would brief the Democratic caucus, then the Republicans right afterward. Gingrich promised that he'd allow C-SPAN to televise Gore's presentation, but reneged, much to our disappointment. The ABC evening news camera caught Gore and Gingrich as they were leaving the caucus after a two-and-one-half-hour tour de force by Gore. The reporter asked Gingrich, "What do you think of the vice president's program to reinvent government?"

"A total success," Gingrich replied.

Reinvention often pushed other issues to the background where Gore was concerned. In January 1997, Gore opened his first meeting with new Secretary of Defense Bill Cohen by saying, "We have a lot of things to discuss, but the *only* topic for today's meeting is reinventing government."

Perhaps the high point of our campaign to educate the government about reinvention came that same month, soon after Clinton and Gore were reelected. Clinton invited his Cabinet to a January 11 meeting at Blair House, the mansion across Pennsylvania Avenue from the White House that served as the president's guest house for visiting heads of government and state. Clinton gave control of the agenda to Gore, and Gore told Elaine Kamarck to arrange for the meeting to educate the Cabinet on reinventing government. "Give them their marching orders," he explained.

Elaine dashed off a list of about fifteen topics and convened the NPR staff. We had two days to prepare papers on each topic that Gore could use to talk from and to lead the discussions. The staff came through beautifully. We divvied up the job among six people and met the deadline with one- or two-page papers on each topic, each filled with real live examples of reinvention from all across government. Gore met with the Cabinet and spent several hours teaching, using our papers along with the inevitable props: a steam trap, a government ashtray, an ancient vacuum tube that was in current use by the FAA to control air traffic, a ruggedized telephone,[4] et al.

The papers we had prepared were well received, and ever since my unexpected success with MIP at DOD, I've believed in building on unexpected successes.

We decided to publish the papers as a book. The president presented in a foreword his case for smaller and more effective government, and explained that the lessons in the book could be a big help in achieving it. Then came an introduction by Gore, and fifteen "chapters" in three broad categories:

I. Deliver Great Service
    1. Identify Your Customers and Win Them Over
    2. Find Out How Things Are Going By Getting Out Of Washington
    3. Be Smart About Information Technology

II. Foster Partnership and Community Solutions
    4. Focus Regulators On Compliance, Not Enforcement
    5. Remove Barriers So Communities Can Produce Results
    6. Use Labor-Management Partnerships and Alternative Dispute Resolution

III. Reinvent To Get The Job Done With Less
    7. Get The Best From People
    8. Look For Reinvention Savings To Fund New Ideas
    9. Pool Resources With Other Departments
    10. Seek Congressional Relief From Wasteful Restrictions
    11. Reengineer To Reduce Headquarters and Overhead
    12. Move Money and Positions To Service Jobs
    13. Use Common Sense Procurement Policies
    14. Expand Competition To Save Money
    15. Create Performance-Based Organizations

Each chapter was very short—the average was 400 words—with tiny stories to illustrate nearly every point. For example, the second chapter offered the following story to illustrate how front-line workers know more about how to improve efficiency than managers in Washington:

> After the White House came up with a legislative proposal to streamline procurement, it was checked out with front-line buyer Michellee Craddock Edwards. She said, "Too bad it won't allow widespread use of the Visa card unless all the red tape is removed from purchases under $2,500." Her great idea became a central part of successful procurement reform legislation and is now saving the nation millions.

We did a lot of polishing. Greg Woods was determined to have a professional and elegant little book that looked great and—most importantly—fit in a jacket pocket. We hired a commercial designer to lay out the book, rather than use the Government Printing Office. Greg joked that it would be America's answer to Mao Tse-tung's *Little Red Book* and researched the size and appearance of the original. I came up with the name, *The Blair House Papers*.

We found a poster from the Cultural Revolution showing dozens of young Chinese leaning out of train windows brandishing the *Little Red Book*. It looked like they were waving *The Blair House Papers*, and that's what we told everybody the poster was.

The Blair House Papers was a big hit. We had 20,000 printed and managed to get them in the hands of thousands of government executives and managers. There is always a lot of curiosity about what goes on at Cabinet meetings, so we had a ready-made market. I took a stack to the monthly meeting of the President's Management Council, where it was customary for the host to supply cookies. I agreed to supply the sweets, which I did: a huge cake in the form of *The Blair House Papers*, complete with Mao-red icing. The council ate up the cake and the books.

Thereafter, at every meeting that NPR had and at most of Gore's, the host handed out copies of *The Blair House Papers*. It became a ritual: the visitors, often subcabinet members or agency heads, would bring their own copy to show they were "with it." It was small enough and short enough that busy executives could read it on the fly; some even read it while being driven to meetings with Gore. Of course, more people carried the book than read it, but even so, lots of people read it. Some of them even followed Gore's reinvention "marching orders."

The 1996 election had gotten me thinking. We had been at reinvention for four years now. I knew that transformation would take a long time. Business leaders had told Gore that it was an eight- to ten-year proposition. Gore had joked that he was committed to spending four years reinventing and if necessary, he was willing to spend four more and four more after that. Now we had the second four years.

It was time to change our thinking and our strategy. I believed—and still believe—that the essence of leadership is to get people to want the goals that the leader wants and then to turn them loose to achieve those goals in whatever way they want. NPR had been a gang of crazy-eyed fanatics doing what they wanted on the way to reinventing government. We found more fanatics all over government who were reinventing in their own way. We had praised and publicized what they were doing and opposed, subverted, and converted their adversaries in the bureaucracy. The arson strategy had been working.

I had been a pretty successful leader of NPR, getting talented people to want what I wanted. Sometimes the process worked the other way: I saw what reinventors in the Environmental Protection Agency (EPA), Customs, or the VA wanted to do, and I decided that I wanted those same things.

We had accomplished a great deal. The federal workforce had shrunk by 426,000 to its lowest level in thirty years, many government customers were being better served, procurement had been radically simplified, some regulatory agencies were winning increased compliance through collaboration with business, 640,000 pages of internal agency rules had been eliminated, and some employees were being empowered.

We had gotten a lot of good press (never enough, but a lot), and some of the academic critics were admitting that maybe there was something to this reinvention thing.

Too much of government, however, had *not* been reinvented. Most agencies were still highly centralized, and some still mistreated their customers and deadened the spirit of their workers. Leadership had taken us halfway there. Now it was time for management to finish the job.

LESSONS FROM CHAPTER NINE: ENCOURAGING AND PROTECTING INNOVATORS

—Delegate some of your authority to front-line workers and encourage them to try new things. Reinvention labs or model activities can produce quick successes.

—Find people who are creating the change you want and make heroes out of them.

—Teach people using examples from their own organizations. They won't easily see the relevance of outside experience.

—Create awards and use them strategically.

—Look for and build on unexpected success.

—Be positive, positive, always positive.

NOTES

1. Air Force Two wasn't quite as glamorous as it might sound. It was a thirty-year-old Boeing 707, long obsolete for airline use and prone to repeated breakdowns that forced Gore to use a more modern but smaller and less comfortable DC-9.

2. Kettl soon became our most informed critic and the most respected outside expert on reinvention. When reporters wanted an impartial view of reinvention, they went to Kettl, and he usually gave us good grades.

3. To their credit, Veterans Affairs soon surveyed veterans and found out they didn't like lines any more than other people.

4. The Navy had always equipped its ships with telephones that were designed and made to government specifications. As part of a broad initiative by the Pentagon to buy commercial off-the-shelf items, the Navy equipped the USS *John Stennis* with commercial phones made by AT&T that cost the Navy thirty dollars. They replaced $420 "ruggedized" phones that were designed to work after the ship sank and was refloated. Gore was fond of saying that a ship would have to be sunk and refloated fourteen times before it made economic sense to equip it with ruggedized phones.

10

The Decline and Fall of a Great Group

(Moving from Leadership to Management)

First we needed to focus on what the job was. Giving orders, or getting the president to give orders, would take us only so far. The problem was that there are at least four possible ways to react to an order:

1. OK, I'll do it.
2. I'd like to do it, but I don't know how.
3. I'll do it if you catch me and make me.
4. What order?

There were certainly some government people in the first category—probably several thousand of the 2.2 million who worked for the government in 1993. But the vast majority of government people at all levels never see nor hear of a presidential order; most of those who see one don't know what it means to them.

The reaction to our customer service executive order is illustrative. Clinton signed Executive Order (EO) #12862 on September 11, 1993. Greg Woods had crafted it, and Greg was as good a writer of plain English as I knew. The EO directed "all agencies" to:

• identify their customers
• ask them how satisfied they were and what they wanted
• post service standards and measure results against them
• compare performance to the best in business

- survey employees about how to give better service
- give customers choices
- make information, services, and complaint systems easily accessible
- provide means to address complaint

It also told agencies to publish their plans and to report to the president.

I thought it was pretty clear, but soon Greg and I were deluged by people asking what to do. I tried telling them just to do what the EO said, but that didn't seem to help them much. Greg realized that if they said they didn't understand, they probably didn't. So he set about to teach them, starting with a conference for executives, then a larger conference for the people from the various agencies who would actually do much of the work to comply with the EO. This approach did a lot of good, but ultimately it was a "retail" operation: we influenced those we touched, and the NPR staff of forty-five could only touch so many.

By contrast, the government was big and diverse, with hundreds of agencies ranging in size from the Postal Service with 870,000 employees to the Christopher Columbus Fellowship Foundation with one. We couldn't work closely with every agency, nor was there any need to. We had to concentrate on those agencies that had a direct impact on millions of Americans.

At the Blair House meeting on reinvention, Gore had told the Cabinet members that he and Clinton expected each of them to set clear specific performance goals for their departments—goals that Americans would notice when they were met.

I had more or less stumbled onto the fact that the Cabinet secretaries and their headquarters didn't have much interaction with the American people; it was the agencies they oversaw that had the direct contact. Thus, most Americans didn't have any interaction with the Treasury Department, except as international travelers dealt with the Customs Service (a part of Treasury) and taxpayers dealt with the Internal Revenue Service (IRS), also a part of the Treasury Department. Similarly, lots of Americans dealt with the Census Bureau, Forest Service, Park Service, or Immigration and Naturalization Service—not with the headquarters of the Departments of Commerce or Agriculture or Interior or Justice, their respective parent organizations.

If we worked directly with these high impact agencies, we could have a big influence on their reinvention efforts. It would bypass the "chain of command"[1] and get directly to the people doing the work. The agency heads would be able to hear directly from Gore (and his trusty NPR staff) what he wanted them to do. The message wouldn't get twisted or diluted as it often did when filtered through departmental headquarters.

We needed to decide which were the agencies with the greatest impact on Americans. I made a list that started with the Postal Service, Social Security, and IRS. Thirty million Americans are veterans, so the Veterans Benefits and Veterans Health Agencies went on the list. Tens of millions visit the national parks every year, so the National Park Service clearly needed to be on the list. Travelers need passports from the Passport Office to leave the country and have to clear Customs and Immigration when they return. Countless millions depend on the FDA to approve new life-saving drugs and to protect them against dangerous new drugs. Then there is the EPA and and and. . . .

Soon our list had thirty-two agencies, including some that most Americans—and even many of the NPR staff—had never heard of.

An NPR staffer named Rick Hernandez wanted to call the agencies Reinvention Impact Centers so they would be abbreviated RICs, pronounced "ricks." That lasted just until we planned the agency heads' first meeting with Gore, and staffers started referring to them as RIC-heads. Clearly that wasn't very uplifting. I wanted the thirty-two agency heads to feel pride in being Gore's chosen team. I didn't think they would aspire to be RIC-heads.

I decided to call them High Impact Agencies, naïvely thinking that the two vowels would make it difficult to turn the designation into an acronym. But throughout government they each became a HIA, pronounced hi-ya. I couldn't prevent an acronym, but at least it didn't sound obscene.

Then I decided that the NPR staff would have to change its spots. Our new business—our only business—was to help the High Impact Agency leaders reinvent and produce results the American people would notice and care about. We would become a consulting "company."

I then proceeded to make the boss's Big Mistake. I assumed that the staff would do what I had decided, just because I had decided it. It seemed reasonable to me, and I guess it always seems reasonable to bosses. After all what *is* a boss except somebody who decides?

I had forgotten my own first principle of leadership: the leader's job is to make people want what he wants, then turn them loose to do their work the way they want to do it, with enthusiasm and creativity. I thought the NPR leadership team—most of whom I loved and loved me—would *want* to do what I wanted them to do, especially when I explained to them why I wanted them to do it.

They were brilliant individuals, and together we had been what Bennis and Biederman described as a "great group."[2] They were extremely talented, driven, wildly optimistic, caring people who couldn't wait to get to work in the morning. In Noel Coward's words, our "work was more fun than fun."[3] They had been doing work they were passionate about, working on things they thought most important, and had recruited like-minded people from around the government to help them.

We had made huge progress over four years by all believing in reinvention and doing what each of us wanted to further it. Now the end of the Clinton–Gore years was in sight. There wasn't a lot of time to figure out what needed to be done and to do it. We needed to be more strategic, more focused on the objective. I had decided it was time to manage.

I assigned each of the NPR leadership team about three to five agencies. Their task was to get close to the agency head, to help him or her decide on and commit to reinvention goals their agencies would meet by September 2000, and then to marshal the resources of NPR to help that agency head reinvent the entire agency.

I chose September 2000 because it was the end of Clinton–Gore's last fiscal year in office and the proper time for a final accounting on reinventing government. It was also—obviously—when the 2000 presidential campaign would be at its hottest and when it would be time for Al Gore to boast of his accomplishments.

For the most part, the NPR team didn't know the agency heads they were assigned to, did not know much about half their agencies, and didn't have a passion for the agency mission. Furthermore, they hadn't asked for the assignment.

They weren't happy.

I wasn't very happy myself. Elaine Kamarck had left government in June 1997 to head a new department at Harvard University, and I was filling in until Gore could get a replacement for her. NPR needed a presence in the Old Executive Office Building where the rest of Gore's staff was located and where Ron Klain, Gore's chief of staff, held daily staff meetings. So I left the bosom of NPR, where my pals were and where the fun was, for the icy atmosphere of the White House complex. It wasn't at all like the TV show, *West Wing*; it was closer to *The Jerry Springer Show*. NPR may have been very high on Gore's priority list, but the political staff mostly distrusted us career civil servants and thought reinvention was a hobbyhorse of Gore's that was irrelevant, or even harmful, to the main act of practical politics.

I needed to get the whole NPR team behind my agenda. I remembered the story of Ralph Stayer and the Johnsonville Sausage Company, where Ralph delegated to the workers the decision on whether the product was good enough to ship. I would hold a two-day offsite meeting at which the NPR staff—not me—would decide on NPR's course.

We found a perfect spot for the offsite: the Xerox Conference Center in Leesburg, Virginia, just thirty-nine miles from the office. As we were planning the offsite, our office manager discovered that we couldn't go to Leesburg because it was too close: a government travel regulation prohibited government workers from being reimbursed for lodging expenses less than fifty miles from their home office.

I pointed out that it would cost more to travel further, but the White House administration office was unmoved. So we found a place for the offsite that exceeded the fifty-mile threshold: the Coolfont Resort in Berkeley Springs, West Virginia, one hundred miles from Washington, D.C. Travel expenses and driving times were triple, costing everybody an extra half day away from the office, but the gods of government travel regulations were assuaged, and the staff was reimbursed for lodging expenses—and an extra sixty-one miles at thirty-one cents a mile.

We might as well have stayed home. The offsite was a total flop. My first mistake was to try to involve the entire staff of fifty people. It was too many people, and their backgrounds were too diverse (from NPR deputy directors who had been at NPR for five years to computer maintainers who had been with us for two weeks) to have any coherent conversation.

My leadership wasn't very inspired either. I appealed to the intellect instead of the heart. I explained that we had accomplished great things so far doing what we wanted, and now we needed to figure out what needed to be done to complete the job, and then do it. I was disappointed when the staff didn't respond positively. Even the leadership team greeted my explanation without enthusiasm. Several to whom I was closest announced, too publicly, I thought, that they had "no energy" for the new approach.

In spite of the failure of the offsite, I pressed ahead. The leadership team grudgingly accepted its assignments and started to meet with leaders of the high-impact agencies, now called HIAs, even by me. The team got the HIAs to commit to reinvention goals that the American people would notice and care about, for example:

- Students or their parents would be able to apply for college financial aid over the Internet and get answers about their eligibility within four days.
- The FDA would cut review times for important new medical devices by thirty percent, speed drug approvals, and assure improved food safety.
- The Weather Service would provide twice as many minutes advance warning of tornadoes and flash floods.
- The IRS would provide tax help by phone around the clock.
- The passport office would eliminate waiting lines.
- The EPA would restore hundreds of brownfields sites—abandoned properties, mostly industrial, with some environmental contamination—to economic reuse.
- The 2000 Census would be the most accurate ever.[4]

We were advancing the work of reinvention through our work with the HIAs, but it was heavy lifting, and we weren't having much fun at it. It was with a long-delayed sense of relief that, in December 1997, six months after Elaine left, I welcomed Morley Winograd, whom Gore had hired to replace Elaine as his senior policy advisor. Morley was one of the rare people who had experience in both politics (he had run Gore's 1992 primary campaign in Michigan) and in business (as regional sales vice president of AT&T). As a bonus, he knew reinvention well and had even covered it extensively in a book he co-authored.[5]

Morley won over the NPR staff after a rocky start. His major sin was that he wasn't Elaine, whom we had all adored. His major virtue was that he cared deeply about the people at NPR, and he showed it.

Along with the stresses of a new boss and a new way of operating, I had imposed the stress of a new office arrangement. It was to be the "office of the future," with modular office furniture ("cubicles" of *Dilbert* fame), state-of-the-art computers and telephones, lots of daylight, and no private offices. To encourage the staff to be more accepting of this new lack of privacy, I gave up my big office (which had captured half of NPR's daylight) and moved to a cubicle. We had the idea of using an office with forty-five workstations to accommodate eighty people. That meant most of us would have to spend substantial time working out of the office so somebody else could work in the office. It also meant we couldn't personalize our own space, because none of us would *have* his or her own space.

Bad idea. "Hoteling"—the practice of coming to work and being assigned to any vacant workstation—didn't work for us. We did manage to squeeze in about ten extra people, but at too high a cost. People like—or need—their own space, and when you take it away from them, it makes them crazy. Some people feel a strong need for privacy and complain loudly when they don't get it. I should probably have sent the malcontents packing, but I procrastinated.

When trying to persuade me to take some difficult action in response to a problem, Greg Woods would often needle me by saying, after he made his recommendation, "Or you could ignore the problem, and maybe it'll go away." That usually spurred me to action, because I knew that ignored problems usually did not go away. The malcontents didn't.

Our abortive attempt at hoteling had another, larger cost. Since the early days of NPR, I had held meetings at 8:30 every morning. The meetings had no name; they were informal, open to anyone who wanted to attend, but normally only the leaders of NPR came. In fact, they self-selected themselves as leaders by attending. There was no agenda; I tried to start with something positive and then each person had a chance to talk about anything he or she wanted to. The meetings were open and honest, with a lot of laughter. If there was a problem, we attended to it; if there was an opportunity, we discussed it and acted on it. We never went our own way as individuals for long, because the meetings kept bringing us back together as a team.

As valuable as the daily meetings were, I felt that I had to make a change. Hoteling couldn't work unless most of the staff spent significant time away from the office. And I could hardly tell the staff to work away from the office if the leadership team did not. And I couldn't expect the leadership team to spend significant time away from the office if I kept having my meetings every morning. So I gave them up for twice-weekly meetings. And since I no longer had an office, they were held in our large conference room.

At about the same time, Morley decided we should organize into teams. At the beginning of NPR, we had a formal hierarchy to manage our 250 people—four deputy directors reported to me, and about twenty-five team leaders reported to them. But after our 1993 report to the president, all but about forty-five people returned to their agencies, and the forty-five worked without much hierarchy—there was Elaine Kamarck, our leader; me, the project director; and John Kamensky and Greg Woods, deputy directors. The rest of the organization just naturally coalesced into informal cells of leaders and followers, with the roles changing from project to project.

Now that we were to have ordained team leaders and nonleaders, fractures began to develop. Some people who weren't ordained thought they should have been; some people who had been free to work on a variety of projects now seemed constrained to support their team; some people who had avoided people or projects they disliked now were assigned to a team and stuck with both.

My morning no-name meetings now became team leader meetings. Attendance was compulsory. Things weren't the same.

By the summer of 1998, our great group had degenerated into a bunch of bickering, distrustful, and disrespectful individuals. We were still held together by a passion for reinvention and—for many of us—by love for each other, but unhappiness ruled. Our work was no longer "more fun than fun." It was more work than work. It was toil.

One day Susan Valaskovic, one of the team leaders, announced that she was tired of everybody being mean to each other and she knew how to change things. She had run into a woman who could help us: Martha Boston, a professional facilitator who had offered to facilitate an offsite for the eight team leaders and me.

Her price—*pro bono*; we would pay only her travel and hotel expenses.[6] I agreed.

Boston turned out to be the most effective facilitator I have ever worked with. She spent an hour or more on the phone with each team leader and two or three hours with me, to prepare for the offsite. She got us to focus on what we wanted to achieve, how we would do it, and how we would relate to each other.

My tendency was usually to concentrate on the "what"—the job that had to be done and let the people issues and the "how" work themselves out, which sometimes happened, sometimes not. Some of the team wanted to concentrate on the people issue—how we treated each other—and let the "what" and "how" issues work themselves out. Boston insisted on working with us simultaneously on what she called the three Ps of success: the product, the process, and the people.

At the end she had led us to breakthrough progress, unlike the failed offsite I had held a year earlier: We wound up recommitting ourselves to our big dream of reinventing government, and we promised to act collaboratively and out of affection for each other. We decided to identify three outcomes that we all would really get behind and make happen. We discarded the notion of "hoteling" in our workspace. People needed their own space, and we would let them have it.

The team finally bought into the idea that we had only a limited time to finish up. Greg Woods electrified us all when he announced that he wanted to "change government forever." We combined this phrase with the idea that—pessimistically (realistically, as it turned out)—we had to finish by the end of 2000; after that nobody would pay attention to us. We calculated that we had exactly 880 days to change government forever. The next day we would have only 879 days to change government forever. Our computer expert arranged for the startup screen on every computer at NPR to display, every morning, exactly how many days we had left to change government forever.

We had mixed success with the three things we decided to all get behind. One was to use the World Wide Web to change government the way Amazon.com had changed bookselling. We succeeded at mobilizing the government behind Web-based services, from tax returns to student loans to campground reservations. Today anyone can go to www.firstgov.gov and access any government information and hundreds of popular services.

The second thing was to get government agencies to work together to achieve results that none of them could achieve alone. We had only limited success in getting, for example, several law enforcement agencies, the Departments of Health and Human Services, Education, and Housing and Urban Development to work together on issues of safe streets. And even with a hard push from the president, we weren't able to get the eight agencies[7] charged with protecting the safety of America's food supply to collaborate to the extent we wanted.

The third thing was transformational. It was getting the high-impact agencies[8]—the ones that had the most impact on Americans—to use a balanced scorecard to measure their progress. "Balanced" meant that measures of performance were combined with measures of customer satisfaction and employee satisfaction. In the long run, no organization could succeed in one of the measures unless it succeeded in all three.

The performance measures would be the reinvention goals that I mentioned earlier. Employee satisfaction would be measured by a government-wide survey on which NPR and the OPM collaborated. Customer satisfaction would be measured with the same instrument used by 164 companies that produce about forty percent of America's gross domestic product: the American Customer Satisfaction Index, produced through a partnership among the University of Michigan Business School, the American Society for Quality, and the CFI Group.

The scores would be published for all to see. The *Wall Street Journal* regularly publishes the American Customer Satisfaction Index, and newspapers across the country pick up its articles. Washington keeps score by media coverage. The best thing that can happen to an agency head is favorable coverage in the *New York Times*, the *Washington Post*, the *Wall Street Journal*, or by network news. The second-best thing is no mention at all. The worst is unfavorable coverage. If we could get the agency scores into the media, it would be catalytic,[9] producing a lasting effect on government long after NPR shut its doors.

It would change the situation I had seen at the Pentagon, which I'm sure is replicated at other agencies. It was standard for the secretary of defense to hold meetings every morning with his assistants for congressional affairs and public affairs. His agenda was driven by what was hot in the news and what was hot in Congress.

My dream was that, all across government, the secretary's morning meetings would one day be driven by progress on the balanced scorecard, instead of progress keeping out of the papers.

As of late 2002, it's still too early to tell whether my dream will come true. At least five of the high-impact agencies use a balanced scorecard and publicize the daylights out of the results. The Veterans Benefits Administration collects and publishes scorecard data for every business line and every field office in the 13,000-person agency. The Postal Service, IRS, and the Bureau of Land

Management are also deeply committed to the balanced scorecard. And until his departure in August 2002 from the Federal Student Aid (FSA) agency, old NPR hand Greg Woods never let a day go by that he didn't talk about FSA's balanced scorecard and about FSA's goal of raising customer satisfaction and employee satisfaction and lowering unit cost.

The press is watching. It has closely covered the American Customer Satisfaction Index results. *Government Executive Magazine*, which is widely read in Washington, regularly researches and grades agency management with the support of a grant from the Pew Charitable Trusts. And Congressional oversight committees are starting to pay attention to measures of agency performance, particularly those required by the Government Performance and Results Act.

There will be a battle over whether to continue paying outsiders like the American Customer Satisfaction Index to collect data that is likely to be embarrassing to some agencies. It's the battle between people who trust the American people to judge government performance and those who don't.

But that's getting ahead of the story. By the fall of 1998, NPR had recovered from my need to manage it. We were no longer a great group, but as Bennis and Biederman pointed out, most great groups don't last very long.[10] We were, however, again an effective group.

While we were falling from greatness, I felt terrible about my efforts to change NPR, which had ended in demoralization. I surely made plenty of mistakes, the principal one being that I became less of a leader as I became more of a manager. But I now believe there just wasn't a way to avoid turmoil and discontent as we made the necessary switch from doing what turned us on to doing what needed to be done. Strategic changes of direction always involve turmoil. My partner at the Public Strategies Group, Chuck Lofy, put it this way:

> Transformational change requires letting go of one way of being before getting to a new way of being. Unfortunately you can't get from the old to the new without stumbling through a period of chaos and confusion.[11]

We had finally found a new way of being that suited the time, considering that we had just 880 days to change government forever. I didn't know it yet, but for me, far fewer than 880 days remained.

LESSONS FROM CHAPTER TEN:
MOVING FROM LEADERSHIP TO MANAGEMENT

—Become a manager when you have to, but never stop being a leader.

—Sometimes the team must switch from doing what turns its members on to doing what needs to be done, but it can't do that without leadership.

—Stone's first principle of leadership: the leader's job is to make people want what he wants, then turn them loose to do their work the way they want to do it.

—The leader must appeal to the heart, not just to the intellect.

—You can't lead an organization through transformational change without stumbling through a period of chaos and confusion.

—Changing the organization's agenda is a big deal. Take the leadership team offsite with a professional facilitator to work it out and buy into it.

NOTES

1. Chain of command is a military term, referring to the line of superior-to-subordinate that stretches directly from the president to the soldier or sailor at the front. It can also be an excuse used in government to keep outsiders—like the White House—from meddling. The concept was meaningless when applied to us, because we gave no commands—we were trying to explain and help people implement the president's orders.

2. Warren Bennis and Patricia Ward Biederman, *Organizing Genius* (Reading, Mass.: Addison Wesley, 1996).

3. Bennis and Biederman, *Organizing Genius.*

4. By and large, the goals were met by the target date of September 2000, although in the presidential campaign Gore didn't claim any of the credit he deserved for them. In one case, the goals had a perverse effect: the Passport Office eliminated its waiting lines by hiring armed guards to keep people from entering the office unless they had an appointment!

5. Morley Winograd and Dudley Buffa, *Taking Control: Politics in the Information Age* (New York: Henry Holt and Co., 1996).

6. Boston was one of an astonishing number of extraordinarily talented people who were eager to donate their time to help us reinvent government. In line with the old saw that no good deed goes unpunished, the White House system for getting reimbursed was so tedious and paper intensive that Boston finally gave up trying to get her expenses paid and absorbed them herself.

7. Food and Drug Administration; U.S. Department of Agriculture; Environmental Protection Agency; Centers for Disease Control and Prevention; National Oceanic and Atmospheric Administration; Bureau of Alcohol, Tobacco, and Firearms; U.S. Customs; and Federal Trade Commission.

8. The thirty-two high-impact agencies are as follows. Within the Department of Agriculture: Animal and Plant Health Inspection Service, Food Safety and Inspection Service, Food and Nutrition Service, Forest Service. Within the Department of Commerce: Bureau of the Census, U.S. and Foreign Commercial Service/ITA, Patent and Trademark Office, National Weather Service. Within the Department of Defense: Acquisition Reform. Within the Department of Education: Federal Student Aid. Within the Department of Health and Human Services: Food and Drug Administration, Administration for Children and Families, Health Care Financing Administration. Within the Department of the Interior: National Park Service, Bureau of Land Management. Within the Department of Justice: Immigration and Naturalization Service. Within the Department of Labor: Occupational Safety and Health Administration. Within the Department of State: Bureau of Consular Affairs. Within the Department of Transportation: Federal Aviation Administration. Within the Department of Treasury: Customs Service, Internal Revenue Service, Office of Domestic Finance/Financial Management Service. Within the Department of Veterans Affairs: Veterans Health Administration, Veterans Benefits Administration. Other: Environmental Protection Agency; Federal Emergency Management Agency; General Services Administration; National Aeronautics and Space Administration; Office of Personnel Management; Small Business Administration; Social Security Administration; and U.S. Postal Service.

9. Jim Collins, "Turning Goals into Results: The Power of Catalytic Mechanisms," *Harvard Business Review* (July–August 1999).

10. Bennis and Biederman, *Organizing Genius*, 216.

11. Private note.

11

To Compliance and Beyond

(Strengthening the Regulatory Process)

Yogi Berra once said, "Baseball's an easy game if you're willing to work hard at it." Reinvention was an easy game for me. I *had* worked hard at it for ten years at the Pentagon. I had developed several themes to guide my way: serving customers, empowering employees, cutting red tape, and fostering excellence. I thought they were universally applicable and set about teaching the gospel.

When I encountered people from regulatory agencies, I would preach the same principles. At the Pentagon, most of the regulations I encountered were internal regulations, which I had come to consider red tape to be gotten rid of. It was usually the right answer, because the vast majority of Pentagon regulations had the effect of keeping people from doing their jobs the way they wanted and because the rulebook rarely was pared; it kept growing and growing.

At NPR, I tried my sermon on Carol Browner, EPA administrator, and the EPA senior staff. It didn't work. Not even close. They didn't think they had customers. They had polluters, and their job was to stop them. Not to say that EPA was alone; one of the NPR staff reported that people at her agency, U.S. Customs, told her, "We don't have customers; we have suspects." A staffer at the Bureau of Land Management reported that their customers were wild horses and burros. And we got a report from FDA that inspectors undergoing training were given T-shirts with "GO FOR THE THROAT" emblazoned on them.

I argued that most businesses wanted to do the right thing, and they should be considered EPA's customers. EPA wasn't buying it.

"We're not like Nordstrom's," one of them said. "We don't provide a product or service that people want. We're in the business of forcing people to do what the law and regulations require."

I thought I had the answer for that one. Steve Guthman, a top executive of Stew Leonard's Dairy, one of America's most customer-friendly supermarkets, had explained why he employed security guards in the stores. "Some of our customers aren't very nice people."

I tried to make the EPA leadership see that, while some of their customers weren't very nice people, most of them were; that is, they wanted to follow the rules or at least were willing to, but they needed help in figuring out how. EPA wasn't buying.

Later when we were trying to get the Occupational Safety and Health Administration (OSHA) to adopt customer service standards, somebody suggested that they start with a promise to be courteous. An OSHA staffer snapped back, "We'll be courteous to THEM if THEY are courteous to us first." So much for the golden rule.

For the first two years of NPR, we mostly ignored the regulatory agencies, and they ignored us.

We did, however, discover a leader in a regulatory agency who had reinvented the way her part of the agency worked. Lynn Gordon was a career executive in Customs, where she served as director of the Miami regional office.

We were looking for reinventors in each department for the vice president to showcase as he traveled around the government teaching reinvention. Lynn was turning Customs upside down.

"When I got to Miami, I found that everybody was suing me," she told us. She went on to explain how, for example, containers of fresh flowers from Colombia were regularly left on the tarmac in the Miami sun for days until a Customs inspector found time to search them for smuggled drugs. By the end of a week, they usually found no drugs—only withered flowers.

Lynn worked out a partnership with Art Torno, managing director for American Airlines in Miami. Lynn wanted to catch drug smugglers, but she didn't want Art's perishable cargo to spoil on the tarmac; Art wanted his shipments to clear Customs quickly, but he didn't want drug smugglers to use American's containers to smuggle drugs. So they made a deal: American would install—under Customs supervision—a surveillance system at its cargo facility in Colombia where the containers were loaded. If American Airlines would make sure no drugs were sneaked into the containers in Colombia, Customs would clear the containers within a few minutes of their arrival at Miami International Airport.

American was happy: their customers got their shipments on time. The Customs inspectors were happy: instead of wasting their time with innocent shipments, they were freed to develop new ways of identifying high-risk shipments. For example, Lynn shifted several inspectors from poking through innocent cargo to a new team using information technology to identify high-risk travelers, such as people who repeatedly took one-day round trips to Jamaica. Seizures of illegal drugs went way up.

Lynn and Art had discovered common ground. By working as partners on this common agenda, both were satisfied.

Patrick Davidson filmed Lynn and Art in the training video that Gore would use to teach reinvention to Treasury employees. We later showed the video, together with all the examples from all the departments, to a focus group of federal employees. The one thing that made them most proud of federal service was when Art Torno said, on camera, "American Airlines is a very satisfied customer of U.S. Customs."

This about an agency where people had said, "We don't have customers, only suspects."

Under the protection of visionary Customs Commissioner George Weise and Deputy Commissioner Mike Lane, Lynn Gordon transformed the entire Miami Customs operation. She slashed paperwork requirements so that, for example, the Greyhound Company, which operated duty-free airport shops, had to file only one form with Customs every *month* instead of one form for every *transaction—700,000 a month.* She transformed passenger processing so that international passengers who posed a low risk of being smugglers got through Customs faster, while the real smugglers got fewer drugs past inspectors.

Lynn was making a difference, but we didn't yet know how to build on her experience.

I had another chance to see reinvention in action early at a regulatory agency. March 3, 1994, was the first anniversary of Clinton's kickoff of NPR, and we used the occasion to stage an event at the White House to attract media attention. We highlighted two federal employees who were successfully reinventing. One of them was Joan Hyatt, an OSHA inspector from Colorado. Joan was chosen for the event by OSHA administrator Joe

Dear, a terrific leader who was to transform the federal agency most business people loved to hate.

Hyatt came to Washington to tell the president (and the media, we vainly hoped)[1] about the first steps in that transformation. She cut quite a figure. I had told her to dress for the White House event like she dressed for work. She showed up in blue jeans, five feet tall and full of energy. Without a trace of nervousness, she proceeded to tell her story to the president and vice president.

OSHA had just slashed its 400-page inspectors' manual, which described in excruciating detail what the inspectors were to do and how to report violations. Hyatt told the president, "I signed up with OSHA to protect the American worker. The best way I can protect the American worker is to walk through a work place and say 'there's a dangerous situation,' and in most cases the bosses would want to fix it. It's just bad business when your workers get hurt."

"But this 400-page manual says we have to treat every inspection like it was going to be a Supreme Court case. Instead of protecting the American worker, I spend my time following the manual, preparing for court cases that never come. With the new ninety-five-page manual, I'm spending a lot more time protecting the American worker and a lot less time on paperwork."

Her little story had profound implications for the whole world of regulation, just like Lynn Gordon's did. But I thought of both their stories as wonderful examples of little steps people throughout government were taking to reinvent, to make government work better and cost less. I didn't yet see that regulatory agencies were a different breed and wouldn't be reinvented by preaching the principles of putting customers first, empowering employees, and cutting red tape.

But we were making progress on other fronts, and we didn't pay any more attention to the special situation of regulatory agencies.

In the 1994 election, the Republicans won control of both houses of Congress. The Republican Party's "Contract With America" called for extensive reform of government regulations. Clinton and Gore wanted to get ahead of the Republicans in fixing the regulatory process. Clinton naturally gave Gore the lead in the administration. Gore recognized some similarity between what the Republicans wanted to do and what he wanted to do. He explained it with a joke.

"We want to fix the process, and the Republicans want to do away with it. It reminds me of the veterinarian who merged his practice with that of a taxidermist. Their sign read, 'Either way you get your dog back.'"

He went about fixing it with his typical deep involvement. He convened the heads of Washington's most important regulatory agencies: EPA, OSHA, FDA, the Federal Trade Commission, the Comptroller of the Currency, the Consumer Products Safety Commission—a dozen or so agency heads—and set about identifying regulatory changes that a Democratic administration could support.

It was slow going at first. There just weren't many bad regulations identified. Then Elaine Kamarck remembered the Lynn Gordon story and proposed that we promulgate a "customer service model" of regulation.

The NPR staff called Lynn Gordon to Washington to help. True to our mantra, we started talking to the customer. We invited people from some major corporations to meet with us and give us their thoughts. Some people from DuPont couldn't be present, so they participated by conference call.

The business people told us they didn't mind the regulations so much, it was the behavior of the regulators they found so objectionable. Lynn described what she was doing in Miami. The people from DuPont were silent during and after her presentation, so someone asked, "What does DuPont think about Lynn's presentation?"

The DuPont people caucused among themselves, then came the answer over the speakerphone.

"DuPont thinks Lynn Gordon should run for president, and if she does, we'll all vote for her."

There was an endorsement of the "customer service model" that any politician could relate to. At his next meeting of the regulatory agency heads, Gore placed Lynn Gordon at the end of the big conference table, where everyone could see her, and asked her to tell her story. When she finished, he announced that he wanted the agency heads to model their enforcement after what Lynn had done in Miami. There was much protest as one agency head after another said it wouldn't work for them. With each objection, Gore turned to Lynn and asked, "What do you think, Lynn?" Lynn refuted all the objections, to Gore's obvious delight.

Joe Dear of OSHA raised a red flag that we did need to pay attention to. He said the people who enforced the regulations, the inspectors, were being evaluated according to the old rules. OSHA graded its inspectors on violations identified and fines levied, not on lives saved, accidents avoided, or hazards eliminated. The other agencies had similar practices. The most egregious was at the Consumer Product Safety Commission, where inspectors were graded on the number of shipments of imported consumer products detained at dockside. Gore agreed with Joe Dear that the system of measurement needed to be overhauled as part of our reinvention.

Most of the agency heads were unconvinced by what Gore and Gordon had said, although Joe Dear arranged after the meeting for his entire OSHA leadership team to go to Miami and spend two days with Customs learning Lynn's approach, then a half day with American Airlines getting the customer's perspective. But I'd guess that most of the others thought Gore had taken leave of his senses. Customers indeed!

The experience gave us enough confidence to order new, wallet-size plastic cards to give out by the thousands. On one side they read, "Reinventing Regulation," with the red, white, and blue NPR logo. On the other side they gave our new four rules for regulators:

1. Cut obsolete regulations.
2. Reward results, not red tape.[2]
3. Get out of Washington—create grassroots partnerships.
4. Negotiate, don't dictate.

They bore the signatures of Bill Clinton and Al Gore.[3]

That became our policy for regulations. Now all we had to do was get it implemented. We concentrated our efforts on four regulatory agencies that seemed the most important to reinvent: OSHA, EPA, FDA, and the IRS.

OSHA had been harshly (but fairly, I thought) criticized by Philip Howard in his 1995 bestseller, *The Death of Common Sense: How Law is Suffocating America* (G. K. Hall Publishing). Howard had poked fun at some OSHA rules that were just plain silly and had made the more important point that most people whose behavior OSHA was trying to regulate never saw an OSHA regulation and wouldn't have understood one if they had seen it. For example, one of the most hazardous occupations addressed was that of construction worker, a job covered by hundreds of pages of rules that no construction worker would ever see. Hundreds of thousands of workplaces employed construction workers, far too many to be inspected by OSHA's meager workforce of fewer than 2,000 people. Clearly OSHA needed another way.

Of the four regulatory agencies we wanted to concentrate on, OSHA was our easiest challenge, because Joe Dear really understood reinvention. One of Joe's first actions was to conduct a GE-style workout,[4] where OSHA workers in the field, like Joan Hyatt, identified the 400-page inspectors' manual as a major impediment to change. Joe agreed on the spot to decentralize authority within OSHA by streamlining the manual, and soon cut it to ninety-five pages.

Joe also discovered, encouraged, and protected Bill Freeman, head of OSHA's Maine office and one of the early heroes of reinvention. The Maine office had won OSHA-wide recognition for having the best record, proportionate to its size, of violations cited and fines assessed. But Freeman recognized that something was seriously wrong; the workplace injury record in Maine was the worst in the nation. He visited Maine's top employers and with their help, came up with a plan called Maine 200. If any of Maine's 200 top employers (in terms of workers' compensation costs) would institute a company safety program jointly staffed by management and labor, Freeman would put them on the bottom of the priority list for scheduled inspections.[5]

Given OSHA's small size, it has only enough inspectors to inspect workplaces on the average of every ninety years, so Freeman was, in effect, offering a free pass for companies that created an effective in-house safety program.

The program was successful. Statewide injury rates fell twenty-five percent, and there were parallel benefits in productivity: at Georgia Pacific, for example, one of Maine's largest employers, the CEO told me they had enjoyed a twenty-five percent rise in productivity, due mainly to rising morale as the workers came to understand that the company cared about their safety.

Maine 200's popularity was limited to employers in the state, NPR, Al Gore, and congressional Republicans. The AFL-CIO and many congressional Democrats hated it because it reduced the number of inspections and fines—the metrics they valued. OSHA middle management hated it because it violated the traditional procedures. Joe Dear courageously protected Freeman and Maine 200 from all the detractors, and with NPR's encouragement, attempted to expand the concept nationwide, only to be slowed down by a lawsuit in which the National Chamber of Commerce successfully claimed that Maine 200 was really a regulation and as such should have gone through the extended formal process for issuing new regulations.[6]

Joe Dear started a lasting change in OSHA when he implemented a national reorganization and training program to convert about half of OSHA's people across the country from inspectors to consultants who would help employers make their workplaces safer.

I was gratified when Philip Howard, OSHA's sharpest and best-informed critic, wrote, "Letting in a little common sense, as found by an OSHA experiment in Maine, has had remarkable results."[7] Perhaps my greatest feeling of satisfaction came at a national OSHA workshop for state directors and union reps when a veteran OSHA compliance officer, Mike Kelly, rose, red-faced with passion for his work, and growled, "I'm AFL-CIO to my bones. I was a union carpenter for twenty years until my wrist hurt so bad I couldn't swing a hammer. So I became an OSHA inspector. You've got to get the AFL-CIO and the other critics off our back. We know the new way saves lives. We'll NEVER go back to the old way."

The EPA represented a different kind of challenge. It was organized, like many federal agencies, around the laws it enforced rather than around its missions or the entities it regulated. Thus, it had a headquarters division devoted to enforcement of the Clean Air Act, one to enforcement of the Clean Water Act, one to Superfund, and so on. Businesses often had to deal with different fiefdoms, none of which had a mission of overall environmental protection. So if a company had a way to drastically reduce air pollution, but at the cost of a slight increase in water pollution, there was no single division at EPA to talk to.

Within EPA, however, there were reinventors plying their trade. In 1995, I traveled to Seattle to present the vice president's hammer award to an EPA-led team that had quickly eliminated a major source of pollution of Puget Sound while saving several hundred jobs.

American President Lines wanted to expand its cargo terminal in the port of Seattle. It was threatening to move its operation to Long Beach, California, because there was no land on which to expand. At the same time, a waterfront plant owned by another company was treating wood with poisonous chemicals to protect it from termites and fungi, and some of the chemicals were leaking into Puget Sound.

EPA stepped in, teamed up with the Port of Seattle, and made everybody a winner. American President Lines got the property they needed by buying the plant and immediately paying to seal the leaks of poisons into Puget Sound. The plant owners got a modest amount of cash for their property, instead of being forced into bankruptcy by EPA enforcement actions. EPA got the pollution stopped in weeks rather than the years it would have taken had it been forced to litigate, *and* the cleanup was funded by American President Lines rather than by EPA. The people around Puget Sound got cleaner water and local jobs were saved.

Another EPA effort stretched the very idea of EPA as a regulatory agency. The voluntary "33/50 Program," started in the first Bush administration, challenged industry to cut environmental releases of seventeen high-volume toxic chemicals by thirty-three percent in two years and fifty percent (750 million pounds) in five years. More than 1,300 companies representing 5,000 facilities signed up and reached the goals a year early, without a single word of government regulation.

The business community had its difficulties with EPA, but it was a raving fan of the agency compared to America's big-city mayors. For years, ever since passage of the Superfund Act in 1980, old industrial properties were being abandoned as their occupants went out of business. It was too risky for anyone to buy or lease the sites, because the law made them liable to clean up whatever (often unknown) pollution may have contaminated the property.

Superfund became a major factor in America's urban decay. The historic cycle of new companies replacing old failed ones in central cities ended. It had become too dangerous to reuse the brownfields sites, so entrepreneurs set up operations on pristine land, far from the city. The jobs were gone; only the polluted sites remained.

In 1993, the Northeast–Midwest Coalition held a public hearing on what to do about abandoned industrial properties in Ohio. EPA assistant administrator Rich Guimond and staff member Marjorie Buckholtz attended the hearing and offered to help. Within a year they had redefined national priorities. EPA took responsibility for helping to remove the barriers to economic use of the vast majority of the 40,000 Superfund sites that posed no threat. They mobilized twenty federal agencies as partners in the effort.

In 1997, when Gore asked the high-impact agencies to set reinvention goals, EPA administrator Carol Browner set a goal of returning 400 brownfield sites to economic reuse by September 2000.

EPA and its partners beat the goal. More than 600 abandoned or underused properties had been returned to productive use by 2000, employing 5,500 people in new jobs in the inner cities.

For the Brownfields redevelopment program, EPA had changed its stripes. In the past, it had ignored all consequences other than environmental. When Marjorie Buckholtz attempted to soften the unintended consequences of Superfund, EPA lawyers admonished her, "This is NOT the Environmental Real Estate Agency," and "This is NOT the Environmental Social Agency." But she pressed on, and eventually EPA won the Ford Foundation's prestigious award for Innovation in American Government for its Brownfields program.

The FDA was another agency that symbolized—to me—the old model of government. Critics called FDA inspectors "jack-booted thugs" when commissioner David Kessler ordered all of Proctor and Gamble's "fresh frozen orange juice" seized, apparently, to protect America from an oxymoron. Other critics pointed out that FDA, in its drive for safety, was unnecessarily delaying the introduction of many safe drugs that could have saved lives.

The critics weren't just in the newspapers. One day my new next-door neighbor, Jeff Gibbs, asked me what I did for a living.

"I'm reinventing government," I answered proudly.

"Well then, why don't you do something about FDA?" he retorted. He went on to describe how FDA was trying to put his client, a small maker of medical devices, out of business for some minor paperwork error on the company's part. I told Jeff to write me a letter, and I would try to help.

I gave Jeff's letter to NPR staffer Jean Logan and asked her to figure it out. She never was able to verify his allegations because of a prohibition against White House interference in the regulatory process, but her digging and listening led her deep into the FDA and its relations with industry. She discovered Ed Esparza, who was developing partnerships with the medical device industry to speed new devices safely to market, and she discovered Marie Urban, who was changing the entire culture of FDA's inspection force from valuing violations found to valuing compliance achieved.

I described in chapter 9 how Urban had started FDA's inspectors on the road to a kind of partnership with those ethical businesses they watched over. Ray Mlecko, FDA district director in Chicago, explained how he decided what businesses were ethical. "If they haven't lied to me, I treat them as ethical."

Merck was an ethical manufacturer of pharmaceuticals. Its mission was to bring relief to people who were suffering with disease. I got to see how seriously Merck's people took their mission when I traveled to Elkton, Virginia, to give a hammer award to FDA and Merck. They had worked in partnership (the "p-word" again, to the consternation of the FDA lawyers) to get the manufacturing process for Crixivan, one of the first medicines effective in treating AIDS, approved in seven weeks, compared to the year or more that approval normally took. Thousands of lives would be saved because Merck and FDA had worked together to speed Crixivan safely to market.

After I presented the award, I was chatting with some of the Merck people who had worked extraordinarily long and hard to meet all the milestones involved in getting FDA's approval. As the deadlines approached, the pressure had become ever more intense.

"I bet you had a heck of a celebration when the FDA approval was announced," I observed.

"Oh, no," came the reply. "Our mission is to bring relief to people who are suffering, and Crixivan takes five weeks to have an effect. So we waited five weeks for our celebration so we'd be celebrating the relief we were delivering rather than the product approval."

I frequently used this story to make the point that people in business were often as driven by idealism as people in government, and that we in government ought not to assume that their motives were base.

FDA had made huge steps forward by recognizing this. It was dramatized for me later in Chicago by veteran FDA inspector Sue Bruederle. Bruederle explained how FDA used to grade her on the number of violations she cited, and now, instead, they tracked how well she fostered compliance with the rules. "They don't even keep track of how many citations I give out."

I tried to trap her. "But sometimes don't you miss the thrill of catching someone doing something wrong?"

Bruederle didn't hesitate for a second. "Oh, no. When I catch someone in a violation, I know we've failed."

I felt positively intoxicated. Here was a reinvention that wouldn't depend on Al Gore or Bob Stone or anybody else. Bruederle, like Mike Kelly at OSHA, had discovered a better way of serving the American public, and she was never going to go back to the old way.

The old way was still the way, however, at the IRS. In the fall of 1995, Gore was addressing the White House Conference on Small Business, a national convention of people who had been elected in state conventions to come to Washington to represent the small business community to the White House. Gore's address focused on the administration's determination to fix the regulatory agencies. He asked the audience a leading question to which the only answer could have been "OSHA," but was answered by a chant that grew louder and louder until Gore couldn't make himself heard: "I-R-S, I-R-S, I-R-S, I-R-S."

Clearly we weren't going to impress the business community by changing OSHA, EPA, and FDA, unless we also brought about change at the IRS. Congress, too, was clamoring for IRS reform.

Now nobody loves the tax collector, and IRS had a thankless job made more unpleasant by the ever-changing, unfair, Byzantine tax code. By tradition, the agency was always headed by a tax lawyer who had some chance of understanding the tax code but who usually had no experience running anything larger that a small law office—not much preparation for leading and managing the 116,000 employees at the IRS.

The IRS had a culture that assumed that what people earned was the legitimate property of the IRS unless they proved otherwise. It graded its employees, like all regulatory agencies did, by counting enforcement actions.

Greg Woods, NPR's deputy director, had a passion to make the IRS customer-friendly. He found an IRS ally in Bob Wenzel, head of the Fresno, California, office, who had served on the NPR staff for its first six months.

The IRS was a particularly tough agency to influence. In fact, it was part of the IRS culture that it was immune to politics—even to politicians who wanted to modernize it and make it more responsive to taxpayers.

Woods had another ally in Elaine Kamarck, who saw the obvious benefits—to the nation as well as to Gore—of fixing the IRS. But the Treasury Department, through Secretary Bob Rubin and Deputy Secretary Larry Summers, wanted no White House interference in IRS business.

Woods wanted to set up a customer service task force after the NPR model, staffed mostly with IRS people and steered by a group that included him, Bob Tobias, president of the National Treasury Employees Union, Bob Wenzel, and me. The group would report to Bob Rubin and Al Gore.

Woods also was insistent that the IRS needed a business leader at its head, not a tax lawyer. Rubin agreed with this and would soon enlist Charles Rossotti, the successful chief executive officer of American Management Systems, to run the agency.

Treasury dug in against a task force. The issue was settled when Kamarck, Summers, and Woods got together for lunch in the White House Mess, a dining room for the exclusive use of White House staff and their guests. Summers proposed a task force made up entirely of Treasury people (including the IRS), reporting to Rubin. Kamarck replied heatedly that Summers' proposal would lead to no meaningful reform and insisted on the Woods proposal. Finally Summers gave in, as any reasonable person would when up against Kamarck's determination.

The task force brought together about fifty of the IRS's most creative people and came up with hundreds of recommendations to make the IRS more customer-friendly while *increasing* revenue.

For example, they proposed to work with troubled small businesses to help them stay in business and avoid future tax problems, rather than seizing their often-meager assets and putting them out of business.

One of Woods' favorite ideas was for the IRS to give a gold card to taxpayers whose returns were unchallenged for five consecutive years—a kind of honor roll. It was too radical for the IRS. What if the taxpayer had really cheated but hadn't been caught? Then the IRS would be issuing gold cards to cheaters. So the gold card never made it into the task force report.[8]

Rossotti and Summers embraced the task force report. The IRS almost immediately extended the hours of its toll-free telephone help line to twenty-four hours a day, seven days a week, and expanded electronic tax filing. It also seems to have figured out how to modernize its 1960s-era computers, although the results aren't all in yet. When its modernization is complete, the IRS will be able to finish the shift from an agency that values only enforcement to one that wins compliance through a continuum of actions: from helping taxpayers who want to comply but don't know how all the way to seizing assets from taxpayers who knowingly evade their obligations.

The IRS reforms should go a long way toward showing Americans that their government has changed. Unfortunately, Gore never got the credit he deserved for the IRS transformation. When the task force report was completed in 1998, Woods and I wanted Gore to trumpet it as a big reinvention success, but we were never able to persuade Ron Klain, Gore's chief of staff, that the publicity would be good for Gore. Klain believed that the IRS was some kind of third rail for Gore to avoid. About that time, Senator William Roth held hearings that spotlighted abuse of Americans by rogue IRS agents and raised a public furor about the need for reform. So most people give Roth all the credit for reforming the IRS.

There is a lot of credit to go around for transformation of regulatory agencies. OSHA, EPA, FDA, the IRS—these are much different now from what they were before NPR came on the scene. A lot of credit goes to Gore, who did so much to encourage change, and to the agency heads. A lot of the credit goes to the civil servants. Most of the changes that I've celebrated had their origins in the civil service. Business, too, deserves some credit for its willingness, in many cases, to partner with government and to try new relationships.

Many of our ideas about reform came from business, including customer service, decentralization of authority, and quality management. I used to think that regulatory reform was different, *sui generis*, with no antecedent in business. But there is an antecedent: the practice of quality control.

Business used to control product quality the way regulators did: inspectors examined the product at the end of the production line. If it was of satisfactory quality, they passed it; if not, they rejected it. Similarly, the old method of government regulatory enforcement had an inspector looking at the end of the process—smokestacks and drain lines in the case of EPA, workplaces in the case of OSHA, and sides of beef in the case of Department of Agriculture meat inspectors. If the result was of satisfactory quality, they passed it; if not, they rejected it.

Then business changed, following the teachings of Juran, Crosby, and Deming. The new business model looked systematically at the entire process: from conception through design, purchasing, manufacturing, and even sales. People went after root causes for defects, found them all through the process, and eliminated them. Now many products meet the "six sigma" quality standard that Motorola pioneered—just over one defect in 360,000 products.

Government is changing in the same way, and the same results are possible.

It matters, because sometimes government wants better and better performance. Not always. The IRS doesn't want you to pay more tax than you owe, and Customs doesn't insist that you bring nothing back from foreign travel. They want compliance with the rules—no more, no less.

But other government agencies aim higher than mere compliance with rules. OSHA, for example, seeks ever-safer workplaces. It's possible for an employer to comply with all existing regulations and still have avoidable accidents. OSHA wants to go *beyond* compliance—as far beyond as six sigma is beyond quality standards that existed twenty years ago. OSHA's new approach will reduce injuries even from unregulated areas—like repetitive stress injuries, or ergonomics.

In March 2001, Congress repealed the ergonomics standard that was issued in the last days of the Clinton administration. There is now no regulation on

ergonomics, but OSHA expects that repetitive stress injuries will decline under its reinvented approach: guidelines, assistance, research, and—as a last
resort—enforcement actions against irresponsible employers under the law
that imposes a "general duty" to provide a safe workplace. OSHA is taking a
systematic approach to safety that parallels business's systematic approach to
quality.

Like OSHA, EPA, and FAA (in fact, any agency concerned with health and
safety) want to go way beyond compliance. The old way couldn't get us there.
The new way can.

The right language to describe the new way still eludes me. In 1997, NPR's
The Blair House Papers encouraged regulators to stress "compliance, not enforcement." That can't be quite right. Enforcement, which in the old way was
everything, is, in the new way, still very important.

The best published treatment of the subject that I've found is by my Public Strategies Group partners, Peter Hutchinson and David Osborne.[9] They
describe the new way as one of "winning voluntary compliance"—which is always cheaper than the enforcement model. The government still needs a big
stick for those who refuse to comply, they say, but most of its energies should
go into educating those who want to comply, making it easier by simplifying
rules and processes, and working in partnership to help them comply.

Hutchinson and Osborne reject the idea that businesses are customers of
regulatory agencies, just as EPA leadership rejected it when I proposed it to
them back in 1993. Hutchinson and Osborne believe that a regulatory
agency's customers are the community as a whole, represented by its elected
officials. They call those who are obligated to comply with the regulations
"compliers." They argue that treating compliers well, assuming that most *want*
to comply, will produce higher levels of compliance. Perhaps that works, and
perhaps we should just avoid the business-based metaphor of "customer" entirely when dealing with regulatory compliance work.

Or perhaps the linguistic difficulty is even more basic. Jean Logan, formerly
NPR's deputy director for regulatory matters, wrote:

> It's not that regulations are necessarily bad; it's just that they are only a tool, one
> of many, and we should view them as such. But once we say "we are regulators,"
> then this tool, this process, defines us. And we won't ever have the future we
> want, if we keep thinking the way we're thinking.[10]

The future that all of us want is one where the aims of government regulation are reached: safe workplaces, safe air travel, a healthy environment, safe and effective medicines, everybody paying his or her fair share of taxes, and so forth. It's a future where honest and law-abiding Americans don't fear or hate their government. NPR has moved us in that direction.

LESSONS FROM CHAPTER ELEVEN: STRENGTHENING THE REGULATORY PROCESS

—Aim to win voluntary compliance—it's always cheaper than the enforcement model.

—Ask inspectors and agents in the field what they need to achieve better compliance.

—Use "compliers" to describe the community subject to regulation and enforcement. Avoid the term "customers," and don't use "violators" or "suspects," either.

—Change compliers' behavior through education, simplification, and partnership.

—Reward inspectors and agents on the basis of compliance achieved.

—Government doesn't have a monopoly on ethical behavior and idealism.

NOTES

1. The media attended the event in the Roosevelt Room—the network anchors were there, and I became excited to think that maybe they were interested in reinvention. But no such luck. When Clinton finished speaking, the only questions they asked were about the latest incident in the Middle East.

2. This was to fix the system for evaluating inspectors.

3. We made unauthorized photocopies of the signatures, because it would have taken forever to get an actual presidential signature. Actually, the White House lawyers would never have let us send such a simple card to the president. I felt comfortable doing that ever since my first meeting with Gore when I showed him my wallet-size card with my principles of reinvention. I had photocopied his and Clinton's signatures then, and Gore had seemed amused by my initiative.

4. GE's CEO, Jack Welch, would meet with front-line workers and ask them what procedures or rules needed to be changed to allow them to be more effective. He would approve the changes on the spot. Welch spread the workout process throughout GE, and it has been widely copied.

5. OSHA performs two types of inspections, scheduled ones in which they do general surveillance of safety in a workplace, and unscheduled ones in response to worker complaints or serious accidents.

6. It surprised me to learn that trade associations sometimes oppose change that appears in their members' interest. I saw the same thing happening when an association of importers opposed Lynn Gordon's reforms at Miami Customs and when the Air Transport Association opposed NPR's consultation directly with the airlines on matters affecting aviation security. Associations often have a stake in keeping relations adversarial between their members and the government. If the relationship became friendlier, association membership might fall.

7. Philip K. Howard, Introduction to *Common Sense Government*, Al Gore (New York: Random House, 1995), xxiii.

8. I later learned that the Minnesota Department of Revenue, under Commissioner John James, had sent thank you letters to people who paid their taxes. They weren't troubled at the possibility—or certainty—of thanking a few cheats among all the honest taxpayers.

9. Peter Hutchinson and David Osborne, "Winning Compliance," *Government Executive Magazine* (June 2000).

10. Jean Logan, Unpublished paper (2000).

Jean Slams the Door

(Facing up to Unpleasant Duties)

I took Latin in high school—four years' worth. My parents made me do it. I didn't get anything out of it. Oh, I learned that natatorium was a fancy word for swimming pool and that canine came from the Latin *cane*, meaning dog, and I did get to feel the breasts of the prettiest girl in Latin class while we were in the natatorium at the Latin picnic junior year, but that's not a lot to show for four years' work.

Years later when I grew to love foreign travel, I decided it had been an opportunity lost not to have studied any live languages. I decided to always learn enough of the language to ask directions, to say please and thank you, and to exchange pleasantries, "The church is very beautiful," or, "This is my third visit to Sicily." It was very hard work, and I often wished I had studied Italian, German, Spanish, and French in high school when I had the chance.

Then one day I realized I had learned something important in the four years after all. I was watching Sir Kenneth Clark on television—the creator of the wonderful 1970s series *Civilization*. Sir Kenneth told of how his parents had forced *him* to take four years of Latin and how valuable it had been.

"I learned something very important that has helped me all through life: There are certain things you have to do even if you don't want to do them."

The things you don't want to do often turn out to be the most important things you've done or the things that make the deepest impression on people.

My pal Jack Crownover was an Air Force lieutenant colonel flying T 39s (the old Sabreliner executive jet) out of Bergstrom Air Force Base in Austin, Texas. Most of his missions involved flying generals and other government big shots around. One day Jack found himself with orders to fly Lieutenant General Chuck Cunningham home to Washington, where General Cunningham served as deputy chief of staff of the Air Force for Programs. General Cunningham was telling Jack how important it was that he get to D.C. because he was to attend a dinner at the White House that night.

Jack looked at the weather forecast, and told the general, "I don't know, sir, there's a whole line of thunderstorms across our path. We may have to land and wait it out."

"You're not listening, Colonel," the general growled. "I said I have to be in Washington this afternoon."

They flew on for a few minutes, and the line of thunderstorms grew more threatening. Jack did something he really didn't want to do. He told the general that he would have to land at Dallas–Fort Worth and let General Cunningham miss his White House dinner. The general was furious.

"I'm ordering you to fly this plane to Andrews!"

Jack's heart was in his mouth, but he managed to get out the denial. "No sir, I'm in command of this plane, and my first responsibility is safety, and I'm landing at DFW."

And that was that, until a few weeks later when Jack got orders transferring him to the Pentagon, Office of the Deputy Chief of Staff of the Air Force for Programs. After Jack moved to this prestigious assignment, General Cunningham called him in.

"Colonel, do you know why you're here?"

"No, sir."

"You kept me from making a dumb mistake. I need people around me who will keep me from making dumb mistakes. That's why I brought you here."

Jack had done something he really didn't want to do, but that he needed to do, and it had paid off for him.

It doesn't always pay off. There's a saying attributed to film mogul Samuel Goldwyn, "I don't want to be surrounded by yes men. I want people to tell me what they think even if it costs them their jobs."

I love to be told how smart or right I am as much as anybody, and in my years as a high-ranking DOD official, I heard a lot of praise, some of it sincere, some not. But when I heard *criticism* from someone of lower rank, I never had to wonder whether it was sincere.

One successful business leader remarked that he made the right decisions only about half the time. His success wasn't due to his brilliant decisions as much as it was to having his mistakes pointed out to him soon enough for him to correct them.

In my early days as a manager, I was embarrassed to admit I didn't always know for sure what was the right thing to do. I thought bosses were paid to know. In 1980, I was assigned the responsibility for determining standards for enlistment into the armed services—a topic about which I was appallingly ignorant, even more ignorant than I had been about tanks eleven years before. Jeanne Fites, an executive who reported to me and knew quite a lot about the subject, told me, "If you're going to be responsible for enlistment standards, you'd better go meet some of the people who are enlisting."

My secret was out! Jeanne knew about my ignorance of the subject, crucially important to my job and—a little more important—to the success of the military. But it didn't seem to reduce her respect for me. This incident, among others, helped me realize that a leader didn't have to know everything or make every right decision. There is help to be had if you're open to being helped.

Years later, in 1993, in the most frantic time at the NPR, I was explaining to an all-hands staff meeting just how we were going to present our ideas to Vice President Gore and his senior team of reviewers. We had a demanding, nearly impossible schedule to meet, but I had a plan. It depended on lots of people doing their parts and a fairly simple—only to me, it soon became apparent—series of draft reports and reviews I called "toll gates."

I explained the process to all assembled, who listened attentively and silently. Jean Logan, a staff member, made her way to where I was sitting, and whispered in my ear, "Bob, these people don't understand a word you've said. You'd better go back and start over if you're going to have any chance of getting them to do what you want."

I wasn't happy, but I was smart enough to know that I needed more people to tell me when I was heading down a wrong path—or heading down a path without any followers. I announced with approval what Jean had whispered to me, hoping that it would encourage others to tell me when I was wrong.

It certainly encouraged Jean. Several months later, after the report had been delivered to the vice president and to the president, with great coverage in the press and on TV, two staff members organized a reunion of NPR "alumni"—former NPR staff who had been returned to the agencies that had lent them to us. The reunion had seemed like a good idea, but it turned out to be a dreadfully gloomy affair, filled with complaints about their bosses, who didn't get reinvention.

I was depressed and wandered into the office of one of the organizers. Jean wandered in to kibitz. I unburdened myself.

"Boy, am I glad THAT'S over! What an awful way to spend an afternoon! That was the most depressing meeting I've ever had to sit through."

I returned to my office, feeling better getting it off my chest, but not for long. Jean fairly flew into my office behind me, slammed the door, and gave me a major dressing down. "BOB STONE, WHAT YOU JUST DID WAS AWFUL! Those people worked their hearts out for two weeks to make this reunion happen, and in ten seconds you totally demoralized them. You should be ashamed of yourself. Now get back there and apologize!" I instantly realized that Jean was right, and I apologized. The apology gave me a chance to tell the people I had hurt how much I valued their hard work and enthusiasm and also to remind them that I, too, had thought the reunion was a good idea. The net result of my insulting them and apologizing was—through Jean's intervention—to raise, not lower, their morale.[1]

I was very thankful for Jean's courageously chewing me out and told everybody about it in the next staff meeting and every chance I could thereafter. When people heard the story for the fourth or seventh time, it sank in that I really did want people to tell me when they thought I was wrong. The staff took to it with some enthusiasm. There were times later that I longed—just for a few seconds—for the old days when people treated the boss as omniscient, but I knew that quick warnings of mistakes made were the surest way to get back on the right path.

My own chance to slam the door when I didn't want to came in Stuttgart, in the fall of 1987, on one of my frequent visits to military bases of all services. By then I was a dedicated practitioner of leadership by encouragement. I believed Goethe: "Correction does much, but encouragement does more."

As a young engineer in the 1960s, my specialty had been diving into development programs that were in trouble and figuring what was wrong with the design and how to fix it. I noticed that didn't make me very popular with the engineers who had designed the equipment that didn't work, but I figured, hey, that's part of my job.

When I came to the Pentagon, my first job was to figure out what was wrong with the Army's program to develop a new tank. I was so successful, I got more and more such assignments. Identifying what was wrong was a talent much valued in OSD, and I was good at it.

I was very stingy with praise. I feared that if I praised someone today, they might take that as an okay to get sloppy tomorrow. It was part of a generally negative attitude I had learned in systems analysis. If I wanted to win someone to my side of an issue, I tried to demonstrate the negative consequences of choosing the other side. Usually our job in OSD was to get the secretary to say no to a proposal from a military department. The negative approach worked pretty well when the objective was getting the boss to say no.

When I took over as deputy assistant secretary of defense for Installations, I continued to point out to people where they were failing. I once prepared a speech to an Army Corps of Engineers group that the DOD public affairs office refused to clear because it was too critical of my audience. I figured that was part of my job.

But my job was no longer getting the boss to say no to the military. I was trying to get the military to change its behavior and adopt excellence as its goal; negativity wasn't winning me many followers.

I described in chapter 4 how I test-marketed my briefing on "Excellent Installations"—my vision for military bases—on Air Force General Larry Welch. He liked it, but said it was too negative. I revised it to take out nearly all the negativity and took it back to Welch.

"It would be great if you just took out the negative stuff."

All I had left in was one chart explaining how the DOD would likely get a big budget cut if it didn't implement my plan for excellence. I was a slow learner when it came to encouragement, but Welch nudged me over the edge. From then on, I tried to be all-positive. If I felt I had to criticize, it became something like, "It's great, and here's a way to make it even greater."

I liked the new me, and people responded very well to my sincerely positive message. Senior military officers joined my campaign for excellent installations. I got endorsements from all the chiefs of staff, from Secretary of Defense Frank Carlucci, Tom Peters, David Packard, and many others.

One day in 1987, I visited Stuttgart, headquarters of the U.S. European Command and paid a courtesy call on Lieutenant General Howard Crowell, an Army general and chief of staff of the command. He got right to what was on his mind.

"Bob, you've seen a lot of bases. How do you think Army bases compare with Air Force bases?"

That was a question I dreaded. It was tough to answer in a positive way. I tried. I mentioned some improvements the Army had made recently, but there was no way to make it positive.

"Air Force bases are better. They're better run, they have nicer buildings, they provide a better standard of living, and they treat people better."

"Why do you think that's true?" Crowell probed. "Is it because they have more money?"

I explained that it wasn't a case of money, but priorities. At bottom, the Air Force cared more than the Army about how its troops were treated and the kinds of places in which they lived, worked, and played—tough medicine to give to an Army general who cared deeply about the troops. Crowell made it a lot tougher on me.

"You know, you would be doing the Army a great service if you would write down what you just explained to me."

"Oh no, I can't do that. If I did that, all my Army friends would be mad at me."

"Well, what's more important," Crowell asked. "Being liked or doing your job?"

I realized that this was a time I had to do something I didn't want to do. I agreed to put my opinions in a letter to him, unvarnished, and let him use the letter with his colleagues—many of whom were my hard-earned and valued friends.

Here are some excerpts from the letter:

When I visited EUCOM last month, you asked for my written assessment of the trends I saw, and of how I thought Army bases compared to Air Force bases (and why). Here it is. It violates my usual style—I much prefer encouragement to criticism. I'm not sure what use it will be to you or to the Army. I would value your advice on what to do next.

Air Force bases look better. Buildings are better kept and freshly painted. Many World War II "temporary" buildings have stucco exteriors that make them look brand new.

Air Force dormitories glisten with pride. The dormitory room is the airman's castle. Army barracks rooms are nobody's castle; they are clearly Army facilities. Some have crude signs stenciled on the wall: "No Smoking in Bed" or other signs that let the soldier know he is an untrustworthy visitor.

Air Force maintenance facilities sparkle. Army maintenance facilities look like "Joe's Garage." In many places there are no maintenance facilities at all. Tens of thousands of soldiers maintain tanks, personnel carriers, and trucks in open fields, which turn to mud in the fall and ice in the winter. When the weather is bad, maintenance is practically impossible. The atmosphere is dehumanizing.

When airmen return from official travel, they can get their expenses reimbursed overnight. While-you-wait service has become standard in several major commands. On Army bases travel expense reimbursement is likely to take several weeks.

Most Army officers agree with the generalizations above. Most ascribe the differences to the Air Force having more money.

It's not money. Paint is cheap, especially if volunteers apply it. The differences reflect what's important to the two Services. The Air Force cares about the appearance of buildings. The Air Force cares about whether an airman gets his money back after a TDY trip. The Air Force cares about an airman's attitude toward the dining hall or the barracks.

The Air Force commander is likely to view his main job as taking care of the airmen; his deputies can take care of the operations. The Army commander views his job as seeing to the mission of the installation; operating and maintaining the base is often beneath him.

A broken toaster in an Air Force dining hall is considered an emergency and must be repaired immediately. The Air Force doesn't want airmen taking a broken toaster casually, for fear they might take a broken airplane casually. In contrast, a broken dishwasher went unrepaired for weeks at an Army base while soldiers ate from paper plates.

How can it be said that the Army doesn't care? After all, it's a bone-deep belief that an officer must care for his soldiers. Caring is taught at West Point, it's taught in leadership courses at all levels: the first responsibility of an officer is to see that the troops have food, shelter, and toilets.

Caring is Army doctrine. (In fact, it is Air Force doctrine too, and has been since the Air Force was the Army Air Corps.) So why does the Army care so little about soldiers' workplaces, time spent waiting for reimbursements, or the other things mentioned previously? And why does the Air Force care so much? Here's a guess: it has to do with how officers in the two services think of themselves and of the people they lead.

Army leaders think of themselves as leaders of soldiers in ground warfare; mud soldiers who in war won't have any need for fancy barracks, dishwashers, well-equipped maintenance facilities, or travel reimbursements.

Air Force leaders think of themselves as aviators, dependent for survival in peacetime and in war on the airmen maintaining the airplanes properly. They fight any hint of satisfaction with imperfection, because they know that imperfection leads to death.

Whatever the cause for the differences between the Services, the Army would benefit greatly by treating soldiers better. Quality leads to more quality. Quality maintenance facilities lead to quality maintenance. Treating soldiers at the dining hall or finance office as though they are important makes them *feel* important. The more important they feel, the better they'll be. The prouder they are, the more they'll accomplish. The Army must make its facilities and base services more like the Air Force. The Army can't afford not to.

That's how I see it.

I've been trying to change things by celebrating loudly every Army triumph over shabbiness, mediocrity, and hassling the troops. Perhaps there's a better way, as you suggest. Perhaps graphically describing the differences between Army and Air Force bases might contribute to a change in direction for the Army, and a commitment to elevate care for its people to the level visible in the Air Force.

Please let me know what you think I ought to do next. My only reservation about the unvarnished truth is that many people close their minds when they encounter it.

The letter turned out to be a bombshell. Crowell sent it to Army Chief of Staff Carl Vuono, who showed it to a few people, who showed it to a few people . . . and so on. A week or so later, I received a note from Colin Powell, then commander of the Army Forces Command in Atlanta, asking if he could see "the letter everybody was talking about."

A few weeks later, I was meeting with an Army general on the forthcoming budget and asked whether he'd seen my letter. "Of course," he replied. "Every general officer in the Army has seen your letter."

Soon the Congress held a hearing on the "Stone letter" and nudged the Navy as well as the Army to aim for excellence on their bases. To top it off, the letter I had been so reluctant to write hadn't cost me any friends. The Army rightly saw it as an act of love on my part—love for soldiers and for the Army. More importantly, it changed the Army. General Vuono established "Army Communities of Excellence," built around the issues I had identified, with monetary incentives up to $10 million for bases that excelled. Army field commanders began to realize their first responsibility was to take care of the troops, and they set about doing it with gusto. The letter got such wide distribution that, a year later, my old friend and colleague, Air Force Colonel Tad Foringer, told me his daughter, Gina, an Army ROTC cadet at Virginia Tech, had been assigned the letter (a photocopy of a photocopy of a photocopy) as part of her ROTC studies.

I adapted the letter for the classes I conducted as part of the courses to prepare officers to command bases in all services. It helped me persuade a lot of officers that the greatest gift a commander could give his troops in peacetime was the conviction of their own worth. It helped me teach them the most important lesson I had learned from Bill Creech: pride is the fuel of human accomplishment.

I'm certain that nothing I ever wrote had so many readers as the letter I didn't want to write, and nothing I ever wrote had such wide and deep influence on the institution of the U.S. Army. In September 1989, after he retired, Crowell wrote me.

> That one letter you wrote to me has indeed caused quite a stir . . . a stir in the right direction. You know, it is interesting how things work. Had you put all that in a memorandum through and to the normal bureaucracy, it might have died a natural death. That it was to an "outsider" carries a certain intrigue and, as in this case, is apt to get a lot of attention. I'd say, well done, Robert—more power to you and keep it up.

LESSONS FROM CHAPTER TWELVE: FACING UP TO UNPLEASANT DUTIES

—Sometimes you need to do things you really don't want to do.

—Facing up to unpleasant duties usually pays off; sometimes it gets you deep in hot water.

—As a leader you'll make the right decisions only about half the time. Encourage others to tell you quickly when you're wrong. And tell your bosses when they're wrong.

—Correction does much, but encouragement does more. So use encouragement always and correction sometimes.

NOTE

1. This is the effect that Disney calls "healing wounds." The idea is that if you heal a wound, even one you've caused, you've made a friend for life. In my case, I know that's true. I once bought a PC from Hewlett-Packard and was very dissatisfied with it. When I asked for my money back after six months, they immediately agreed. Next time I'm in the market for anything they make, I'll look favorably on anything made by HP. They healed my wound.

13

Junkyard Dogs

(Avoiding Inspector Generals)

My Uncle Harry was in and out of a number of businesses—coal, junk, rental properties, and poker playing. While he was in the junk business, he had a junkyard dog named King. King was huge and mean. I never knew him to actually bite anybody, but he scared the daylights out of anybody he wanted to. He didn't like my fourth-grade playmate Norton Horowitz, so he followed Norton home from school one day and parked himself in front of the Horowitz house.

King would snarl at anyone trying to approach the house. For twenty-four hours he stayed, deterring the milkman, the mailman, and everybody else from entering or leaving. Finally Mr. Horowitz had to call Uncle Harry and plead with him to set his family free by taking King away.

Years later, in 1981, when President Reagan signed the amended Inspector Generals Act, he said that the IGs were to be "as mean as junkyard dogs." I knew just what he meant. He meant as mean as King.

By and large, they have lived up to their billing. They're mean, and they scare the daylights out of everybody they snarl at. They snarl mostly at the good guys who challenge the status quo or who make a mistake.

My first exposure to the DOD IG wasn't scary—it was an episode out of *Keystone Kops*. I had heard that somebody in my organization had filed a travel request to visit a DOD operation in the Philippines, then exchanged his ticket for two tickets to San Francisco, where he vacationed with his girlfriend at government expense. I called the IG into the case, supplied him with approximate dates, and told him the sources of my information. Months went by, the trail went cold, and the suspect escaped.

My next exposure to the IG was a little scary. I've already recounted in chapter 2 the story of the DOD construction manual, the little yellow book, and how I had printed it at private expense and issued it over the IG's objection. A DOD directive, number DODD 4270.1, gave me authority to issue a construction manual after "coordinating" it (i.e., circulating it for comment) around the department. Since there are often disagreements, directives usually provide for resolving them. In this case, the directive gave me the authority to resolve disagreements.

So when the IG, among others, objected to the draft manual, I resolved all the disagreements in my favor and issued it.

The IG struck back, and he played dirty. He wrote to Will Taft, the deputy secretary of defense, that I had exceeded my authority in issuing the little yellow book.

That's a serious charge, in some ways more serious than exchanging an airplane ticket to Manila for two tickets to San Francisco and taking your girlfriend on a government-paid vacation. Civil servants exercise the power of the U.S. government, and they must act within their authority or our American system of law and administration breaks down.

I thought I was on safe ground, because my lawyer from the DOD general counsel's office, George Schlossberg, had signed a coordination sheet confirming that, in his view, which itself was authoritative, I was within my authority. I assumed that when Will Taft got this empty accusation from the IG (with whom *he* had his own bitter disagreements), he would pin a medal on me or at least take my side.

But instead Taft sent the IG's accusation on to Bob Costello, my boss, who was already furious with me over the manual, to be sorted out with the general counsel's assistance.

The news still wasn't bad, I thought, since George Schlossberg would confirm what he already had agreed to, namely that I did have the authority. However, George's boss took him off the case. George did secretly help me frame a set of lawyerly questions for Costello to ask the general counsel, questions that could only be answered in my favor. And so the general counsel and Costello reported to Taft that I had indeed acted within my authority. I had escaped, but only after being as scared as Norton Horowitz when King chased him home from school in the fourth grade.

I had only been threatened with firing, and the odds were pretty remote, although not remote enough to make me comfortable. Much worse is the way the IG can turn an innocent mistake by an ethical person into a threat of criminal prosecution.

One day a young government manager working with my office—let's call him Fred—asked to speak privately to me. Fred was near hysteria. The IG had decided he had committed a crime and was recommending to the Justice Department that it prosecute him.

Fred had bought a house a couple of years before and had borrowed money to furnish it from a close friend who was also a subordinate. It's against the law for a government worker to borrow money from a subordinate, but Fred's offense was leavened (in my opinion) by three facts: (1) it was a close friend; (2) Fred didn't know it was against the law; and (3) the friend was in the process of leaving the government for the private sector. Not much of an offense, any reasonable person might say.

Fred compounded his mistake two years later when he filled out the financial disclosure report that many government employees labor over. The form is so complicated that I've never done it correctly the first time. I've always forgotten some mutual fund sale, or Roxane's 401K, or something. Fortunately for me, the DOD ethics office went over the forms very carefully and checked and cross-checked every entry against the previous year's form and always gave me a chance to straighten it out before the IG could go after me. Unfortunately, Fred forgot to list the loan and didn't get a second chance.

I later got to know Fred well and found him to have as strict a sense of honesty and integrity as anybody I have ever worked with. He once went to a ballgame with me, but only after making sure that I didn't intend to buy a ticket from a scalper, because scalping was against the law. He had a spotless ten-year record of government employment. There was no way Fred would have intentionally falsified the financial disclosure form.

But the IG put him through hell because that's what the IG does, and that's what the IG is graded on by Congress and the public. The IG counts scalps, and to them Fred was a scalp.

Fortunately, saner heads at Justice refused to prosecute. Fred's agency head then met with me to decide how to respond to the IG, who was now recommending that Fred be fired. I argued that it was a simple mistake that didn't warrant any more than a don't-do-it-again letter of admonition, but the agency head thought this would be seen as a slap in the face of the IG, which he was afraid to administer. Instead he decided to reduce Fred one grade.

Fred's story had a happy ending if you don't count the legal fees he incurred and the demotion and the anguish he went through worrying about his career and possible incarceration.

I have known many dedicated, highly ethical civil servants who have been subjected to abuse by IGs. Fred is far from unique in being recommended for firing.

Another civil servant I respect highly—call her Erin—let a contract to a firm that promised to help her stop the theft of thousands of dollars worth of bar drinks at a military club she was responsible for. Someone phoned in an anonymous call to the IG that the contract award was an act of nepotism. (Erin always suspected that the anonymous accusation came from the person she suspected of stealing the drinks.) The IG found no nepotism, but found (from Erin) that the contractor wasn't performing up to the contract. Recommendation: Erin should be fired. Again, as in Fred's case, her base commander had some common sense that the IG lacked. He wrote her a "don't-do-it-again" letter that was kept in her personnel file for a year, then destroyed.

She was furious at the injustice of the letter, but at least it put an end to the months of anguish and legal expense she suffered while she wondered whether the base commander would have the guts to defy the IG's recommendation.

Federal employees at town meetings with the vice president repeatedly complained that they had been hounded by IGs whenever they had tried to do things differently than the way they had always been done. This is perhaps the major "contribution" of the IGs: stifling innovation.

Part of the problem is the IGs' charter to identify "waste, fraud, and abuse." The IGs have no institutional expertise to identify waste and usually no relevant management or leadership experience[1] on which they can call to distinguish between wasteful and cost-effective expenditures.

When Secretary of Defense Frank Carlucci asked the DOD IG to look into how the military was spending the $30 billion that the Reagan administration had added for readiness, the IG floated a report that a crazy general was spending the readiness money on paint. The "crazy general" was Bill Creech, and the million dollars or so he spent on paint was critical to his success in doubling the combat capability of a 200,000-troop command. But to the IG it was waste.

Waste is a management responsibility. Managers are appointed to manage. Absent fraud or abuse of office, it should be up to them to define what is wasteful and what is not. If General Creech insisted on painting the backs of stop signs brown (and he did), he should be judged by how TAC performed, not on how many dollars he spent on paint.

As deputy assistant secretary of defense, I worked fanatically to get the military leadership to provide excellent places to work and live and excellent base services for the soldiers, sailors, marines, and airmen who defend America. Every step of the way, the IG and its soul mates in the audit agencies opposed the struggle for excellence as wasteful, just as they considered Creech's paint wasteful.

For example, Dick McSeveny, a facilities manager in Marine Corps headquarters, was hounded by the Naval Audit Service for trying to obtain modern barracks for Marines while there were plenty of depressingly run-down (but not yet fallen down) barracks available. Only when I insisted that McSeveny was doing what the secretary of defense had directed did they get off his back.

Fraud and abuse are a different story. There are people who steal from the government and people who abuse their office. Public confidence in government, as well as morale among the honest workers, demands that we go after them. That could be a job for the IG. Unfortunately, it's one that I have no confidence that they do effectively.

There is an old saw around the Pentagon that the IG comes around after the battle and shoots the wounded. But George Schlossberg summarized it better. He suggests that Theodore Roosevelt's words fit the IG:

> It is not the critic that counts, nor the man who points how the strong man stumbles or where the doer of deeds could have done them better. The credit belongs to the man who is actually in the arena, whose face is marred by the dust and sweat and blood; who strives valiantly; who errs and comes short again and again because there is no effort without error and shortcoming, but who does actually strive to do the deed; who knows the great devotion; who spends himself in a worthy cause, who at the best knows in the end the triumph of high achievement, and who at the worst, if he fails while daring greatly, knows that his place shall never be with those cold and timid souls who know neither victory nor defeat.

George concluded, "I think this sums up the IG concept perfectly. We have prosecutors for wrongdoers and Congress to second-guess government officials. What benefit is there from an entity in an otherwise decisive organization that makes decision makers hesitate? I thought we learned all we needed to learn about IGs from watching political commissars in the USSR.

LESSONS FROM CHAPTER THIRTEEN: AVOIDING INSPECTOR GENERALS

—IGs are graded on people punished and dollars wasted.

—IGs often play dirty.

—IGs often turn innocent mistakes into high crimes.

—It takes courage to oppose an IG's recommendation.

—Agency heads fear to oppose the IGs, even when they think the IG is wrong.

NOTE

1. These remarks refer to IGs in the civilian agencies. The military departments often assign people with extensive operational (and often command) experience to IG positions and rotate people in and out of IG jobs. The civilian IGs, on the other hand, can serve their entire careers in the IG organizations.

Overcoming Success

(Getting Past the Barriers to Change)

The 1999 St. Louis Rams were on top of the football world. They had just held off the Tennessee Titans, 23–16, thanks to Mike Jones' game-saving tackle of the Titans' Kevin Dyson at the Rams' one-yard line as time ran out. The Rams were the 1999 Super Bowl champs.

It was the end of a dream season. The Rams had won thirteen games and lost only three in the regular season and then swept the Vikings and Buccaneers in the playoffs. They had scored 526 points—third highest in league history.

After a little time to savor the championship, the Rams organization—executives, coaches, and players—looked forward to the 2000 season with every expectation of repeating their success. It would be tough, no doubt, but the 1999 season had been tough, too, and they had come through.

But it wasn't to be. The 2000 Rams had a decent season; they even outscored the 1999 champs by fourteen points. But they barely made the playoffs with a 10–6 record, and they lost to the lowly New Orleans Saints in the first round. It was a big surprise.

It shouldn't have been. The Rams were the twenty-eighth of thirty-five Super Bowl winners to fail to repeat. In fact, they joined a majority (nineteen of thirty-five) of winners who didn't even make it back to the Super Bowl the next year.

I researched these statistics after a failed attempt to teach reinventing government to a seminar at the Federal Executive Institute. The high point for the recalcitrant students, and the low point for me, came when a woman from the

Naval Sea Systems Command, extremely confident about the caliber of her organization, screamed at me from the back row, "WE WON THE SUPER BOWL LAST YEAR. WHY ARE YOU TELLING US WE HAVE TO CHANGE?"

If I had known the statistics, perhaps I could have convinced her. Her sentiment isn't uncommon in government.

When Greg Woods was installed as chief operating officer of the Federal Student Aid agency of the Department of Education, he was charged by law to raise customer satisfaction and to cut costs.

It would have been easier had the student aid apparatus been an obvious shambles, but the agency had already helped over 30 million Americans finance their higher education. As one staff member—albeit more politely but just as frustrated as the woman who had yelled at me—put it, "Who is this Greg Woods to come in and tell us we have to change? We've been getting the loans out since long before he got here, and we'll go on long after he's gone."

Woods was facing the Super Bowl barrier. His biggest hurdle was the past success of the organization.

It's the barrier every government leader faces. After all, the U.S. government *does* work. In many ways, it is the envy of the world—at least the world beyond our shores. It collects the taxes, it gets out the social security checks, it polices the environment, and it regulates the financial markets. Like the St. Louis Rams, the U.S. government had a decent year in 2000—and every year—"good enough for government work," as the old saying goes.

It's easier to mobilize people for change if things are obviously *not* good enough for government work. When I became deputy assistant secretary of defense for Installations and looked around the defense world, I saw shabby buildings, poor services, and troops struggling in shameful conditions, like the thousands of soldiers who had no place to maintain their military vehicles— tanks, howitzers, and trucks—except in a lot covered with thick, sucking, oozing mud. Military leaders had a tough sell to convince those troops they were America's elite warriors.

Whenever I was tired or up against people who wanted to divert funds away from construction, visions of these troops struggling in the mud gave me energy to keep at it.

Soon after I took over, a tragedy hit the Army. A twelve-year-old son of a soldier assigned to Fort Ord killed himself. His family had been living in their car, and he left a note saying that perhaps his death would make it easier for the family to find suitable housing. His death spurred Army Colonel Fred Meurer to invent new ways to provide housing for soldiers with families. It also inspired George Schlossberg, then a new lawyer in the ultra conservative defense general counsel office, to come up with ingenious new interpretations of the construction statutes to permit us to provide housing much faster than the five to eight years it normally took. Schlossberg has now been in private practice for ten years, but to this day, the incident brings tears to his eyes, and he donates time to helping the military provide excellence for its people.

Even as bad as the situation was for the troops, the engineers in charge of providing Army facilities thought they were doing well. Not Super Bowl winners, perhaps, but as well as could be done. I shamed them with the first story I ever told as part of my job.

I had heard the story from Warren K. "Doc" Lewis, the father of chemical engineering in the United States and an inspiration to me in my days at MIT. A young engineer, newly hired in a steel mill, was assigned to look around and learn how the plant worked. He soon stumbled onto the fact that the blast furnace was dependent for cooling on a single pump. If the pump failed, there would be millions of dollars in damage.

He told his new boss, then his boss's boss, but they brushed him off. Undaunted, he kept telling people up the line, but to no avail. He finally got to the plant manager, who also brushed him off.

Soon afterward, the pump failed, and the blast furnace was wrecked. The plant manager called in the young engineer and fired him.

"But I tried to warn you how critical a pump failure would be."

"If you knew, you should have *made* me listen."

I told the Army engineers it was *their* fault for not making the people who controlled the money listen. This little story helped inspire some Army officers to fight successfully with their colleagues and their superiors for an increased share of the defense budget they needed to take care of the troops.

At defense, I inherited a situation that I recognized as shameful, and I tapped people's sense of shame to get them to want to change. There are other senses to tap, including pride, embarrassment, duty, fear, hope, and most important of all, the desire to make a difference.

It's a task for the leader to recognize the need for change and to get people to embrace it.

George Bernard Shaw contrasted two kinds of people. "You see things, and you say, 'Why?' But I see things that never were, and I say, 'Why not?' "[1]

The leader needs to combine both visions into one.

In 1993, Vice President Gore saw both what is and what could be. He recognized the need to change government. As a politician, he was especially sensitive to Americans' declining trust in government—from seventy-five percent in 1963 to less than twenty percent by 1993. He saw this decline as a demand for change in the way government works.

There was nothing new in Gore's recognition of what is, or in his desire for change. Every new administration since Eisenhower had announced the need to change government. They all brought in outside "experts" who catalogued needed changes. They issued a few executive orders and then went on with business as usual.

Gore decided that his job was to make people *want* to change. He collected a long list of props that symbolized the need for change, starting with my old steam trap, which epitomized the ludicrous inefficiency of the procurement system and its distrust of non-"experts" to buy anything. He also enjoyed showing off the Small Business Administration's one-sheet loan application and the thirty-page application it replaced. And when he brandished a 1950s-era vacuum tube, still being used in the FAA's air traffic control radars, people—especially air travelers—gasped.

But Gore realized that steam traps and vacuum tubes weren't enough. People wouldn't jump out of bed in the morning and rush to work to make it easier to buy steam traps. He didn't just want to fix what was: he wanted what never was. He appealed to our pride, our hope, and our desire to make a difference.

Whenever he spoke to government employees, he would wind up his plea for reinvention with a challenge. "Made in Japan! That used to be a sign of poor workmanship, of cheap materials, of low quality. Now it means excellent workmanship, the very highest quality."

Then he would curl his lip and sneer, "Good enough for government work! [long, long pause] How does it make you feel when you hear that?"

"But just as the meaning of 'made in Japan' has been turned upside down, we can reverse the meaning of 'good enough for government work.' We can once again make it mean what it used to mean—only the best, only the very highest quality."

Even that wasn't enough for Gore. Making it easier to buy steam traps wasn't enough and neither was restoring pride in government service. Gore summoned all public servants to a higher calling. He told us the whole future of self-government was at stake, for if people didn't see that government could help solve their problems, they would turn away from government. He made us believe it was our mission "to redeem the promise of Philadelphia."

None of the thousands of government workers who heard Gore summon them and none of the tens of thousands who saw him on video ever doubted that they needed to change. He had overcome the Super Bowl barrier.

The IRS was facing its own Super Bowl barrier. America's tax collector was arguably the best in the world, with the highest rate of voluntary compliance with the tax law. When anybody commented on the unpopularity of the IRS, the response was, "well you can't expect people to love the tax collector."

I described in chapter 11 how Greg Woods drove to completion the idea of a customer service task force of IRS employees working to define how the IRS could improve service to the taxpayer. The task force followed the model of NPR—in-house employees from all levels, from executive to frontline worker, some invited for their known dissatisfaction with the system and some troublemakers volunteering for a chance to get out of sight for a while.

Greg handpicked the task force leader, Bob Wenzel, a universally respected IRS career executive who ran the IRS Fresno center and who had served on the NPR staff. Wenzel and his team saw things as they were, as well as the way they never were. The task force met with individual taxpayers, tax preparers, leaders of businesses that excelled in customer service, and leaders of other agencies undergoing change. It came up with more than 200 recommendations for change, starting with proposals to hold monthly problem-solving days and to extend telephone service to seven days a week, twenty-four hours a day.

The new commissioner, Charles Rossotti, who was the first IRS head to come from the business sector rather than the ranks of tax attorneys, adopted most of the recommended changes.

Greg Woods left NPR to head the Federal Student Aid Agency, where one of his first acts was to establish a customer service task force on the NPR and IRS models to identify things as they were and as they never were but might be. The task force strengthened the case for change in the Federal Student Aid Agency and served, as had its predecessors, to help overcome the organization's Super Bowl barrier to change.

Seeing things as they are is not a trivial task. General Larry Welch commanded the Air Force's Strategic Air Command before he became chief of staff in 1986. He admonished all his installation commanders to look around very carefully the first few days they were at their new posts, because after a short time they would lose the ability to see things as they are.

Welch helped prove his point in a conversation with me one day when I was arguing for the importance of MIP as a crucial weapon in the war on stupid bureaucratic rules and procedures. Welch said that the Air Force had long since won that war—maybe the Army still needed to, but not the Air Force.

I searched for an example and came up with a nonsensical procedure the Army had just identified and eliminated: the need for a special government driver's license for anybody who drove an Army vehicle, even if they had a valid state license.

Welch broke out in a wide grin, reached into his back pocket, and pulled out his wallet, from which he extracted a small card and handed it to me. It was his government driver's license.

From that point on, Welch was the number one supporter in all of DOD for MIP and a relentless force for decentralizing, deregulating, and delegating authority in the Air Force.

A task force with diversity of age and rank would have no trouble identifying the government driver's license as crazy. I've always charged task forces with the advice of my favorite military engineer, Air Force Major General Jud Ellis, now retired: "Don't do any dumb things on purpose; we do enough dumb things by accident."

Besides fresh eyes, another important advantage that young low-ranking people bring is their firsthand exposure to bureaucratic micromanagement and abuse. Former Air Force Lieutenant General Leo Marquez used to play a little game with new colonels assigned to the Air Staff. "Have you noticed," he would ask, "how all the problems that bothered you when you were captains have been solved?"

Of course the problems had not been solved; the only change was that the colonels could now pull rank to overcome the old problems. From this experience I coined the Marquez rule: When victims of bureaucratic abuse finally advance to a position where they can do something about it, they usually decide instead that it is their turn to practice it.

Perhaps that was why most of the students in my disastrous Federal Executive Institute seminar had been so turned off by the prospect of change. Fortunately, however, not all of them were. Four of the fifteen students had really signed up to learn about reinventing government; the others turned out to have been prisoners, involuntarily assigned to the reinvention seminar when their first, second, and third choices filled up.

The students decided (with a little urging from me) to split into two groups: Group One comprised the Super Bowl winners, the people who believed that things were basically OK and no major changes were needed or wanted in their organizations; Group Two believed that transformational change was necessary and wanted to work on ways to overcome barriers to transformational change.

My teaching partner was Lorraine Chang, a partner at the Public Strategies Group, who was far more talented than I in dealing with recalcitrants. She got Group One. I got Group Two, the four who believed that change was necessary and wanted help in dealing with it.

As so often happens to teachers, I learned more from the students than they learned from me. They identified what they thought was the number one barrier to change. They called it the attitude of "We don't need to *keep* changing," sometimes expressed as, "We're not as bad as you think," or "We're no worse than anybody else."

The group came up with a pretty good list of actions to overcome the Super Bowl barrier:

- Clarify the reasons change is necessary. They might include externally driven factors, like demand for more speed, lower budgets, or higher customer expectations.
- Spell out the consequences of failing to change. They could include job loss, loss of business to the private sector, or letting down people they were committed to (as in the case of Naval Sea Systems Command, the sailors).
- *Show* successes in your organization and in others. Take your people to see best practices. Bring them face to face with successful change.
- Similarly, bring them face to face with customer expectations. Bring customers to the workplace, send employees to see customers in their environment, and conduct surveys.
- Celebrate every little success.

- Provide a security blanket. Assure people you'll keep what's good in the organization and acknowledge their contribution and past successes.
- Remove fear of failure; reward learning from mistakes.
- Remove fear of job loss.
- Spend lots of time with change agents in the organization for their ideas and for the energy and optimism they foster.

Not a bad checklist for any leader who is trying to overcome success.

LESSONS FROM CHAPTER FOURTEEN: GETTING PAST THE BARRIERS TO CHANGE

—It's the leader's job to recognize the need for change and to get people to embrace it.

—The biggest hurdle is the past success—real or imaginary—of the organization.

—It's easier to mobilize people for change if things are obviously going poorly.

—Touch people's hearts to get them to want to change. Tap into their sense of pride, shame, embarrassment, duty, fear, hope, and most important of all, their desire to make a difference.

—Set up a customer service task force on the NPR and IRS models to make the case for change.

NOTE

1. *Back to Methuselah, Part I, Act I (1921)*. Edward Kennedy, speaking at Robert Kennedy's funeral, quoted Robert as saying, "Some men see things as they are and say 'Why?' I dream things that never were and say 'Why not?' "—St. Patrick's Cathedral, New York, June 8, 1968.

Ten Lessons in Leadership

When Vince Lombardi took over as coach of the Washington Redskins in 1970, the fun-loving Redskins star quarterback, Sonny Jurgenson, didn't know what to expect from this stern disciplinarian.

He was relieved when they met and the great coach told him what he expected of Jurgenson. "Be yourself."

That's probably the best advice I can give anyone about leadership. In thirty years of government service, I learned ten things besides "be yourself" that should be useful to anyone trying to transform his or her part of government— or any other place of work.

1. BE PLEASANT

If you're going to be a leader you're going to need a lot of help. Start by being pleasant. If you're not naturally pleasant, fake it. It'll soon become natural.

At NPR, I bought an espresso machine and made cappuccino for myself and for anybody nearby. People told me a lot because I made cappuccino. If there was bad news—or better, if there was good news—nobody ever hesitated to bother me because they thought I was too busy. After all, I had plenty of time to make cappuccino, didn't I?

I once attended a company Christmas party where the CEO made a short speech about how he valued hearing what was on people's minds, which was why he had an open door policy. "Don't be put off when you see my door closed, though," he explained. "I generally keep it closed so I can have some quiet." I don't think many people took advantage of his "open door" policy.

Be careful if you have an assistant—some assistants are wonders at inhibiting people. Twice I worked for bosses who had military assistants so unpleasant that I hated to call my boss for fear I would have to talk to the assistant. My bosses missed getting some advice that they could have used. Another time I had a secretary who told people that I was too busy to see them if she didn't think they were important. It took me too long to find other work for her.

If you're pleasant, good things happen even when you don't plan them. Once while in OSD, I needed a big favor from the Army Corps of Engineers, and I racked my brain to think of what I could do in return. I finally told Major General Pete Offringa, assistant chief of engineers, that I was trying to figure out what reason I could give him to do it. "I don't need a reason," he replied. "I'll do it to help the team."

Being pleasant can start a virtuous circle—people respond by being pleasant to others and to you. In the Pentagon, Gerry Kauvar joked about running a "favor exchange." He did favors for people partly because that's the way he was and partly because he knew that some of them would be repaid with interest.

2. BE TRUSTING

Trust is a capital asset.[1] People who are trusted are happier and more productive in their work—and more trustworthy. Henry Stimson said, "The way to make a man trustworthy is to trust him."

Yet mistrust is endemic in government; in fact, it's almost universal policy. Government employees, by and large, aren't trusted, for example, to buy things or to decide when and where they need to go on business trips. They need approval from bosses and checkers. Government doesn't trust the bosses either; that's why there are IGs to check up on them.

At the Reinventing Government Summit in Philadelphia in 1993, Patrick Mene, vice president of Ritz Carlton, told Gore that Ritz trusts *every employee* with $2,000 of spending authority on behalf of a customer, no questions asked. Gore asked what Ritz did if it caught somebody abusing the trust. The response: "I don't know, we never have."

At NPR, I insisted that staff members could travel whenever and wherever they chose, no approval needed. Maybe someone sometime took a trip that wasn't necessary, but the cost would have paled next to the benefit in spirit that came from everyone feeling trusted.

Of course, *be* trustworthy: speak your mind, tell the truth, keep your word. Just as being pleasant can start a virtuous circle, so can trusting and being trustworthy. And to preserve the virtuous circle, don't waste a lot of energy on people who aren't both trusting and trustworthy, and don't keep them in your organization.

3. BE BOLD

Leadership is about movement. It's about causing others to go somewhere different. It's very different from management. Management is about stability, about operating things as they are, minimizing mistakes, making small improvements.

So if you're a leader you've got to *move*.

Moving, however, can get you into trouble, and people will try to protect you by advising you to stay *out* of trouble. Make sure you have people on your team who will *keep you* from staying out of trouble.

When President Clinton was planning to announce that the federal government would take the lead in hiring people on welfare as an example to business, the experts in government said it couldn't be done—the law mandated hiring preference for veterans, people on welfare didn't have the skills or work habits that federal jobs require, managers would resist, and so forth.

NPR deputy Susan Valaskovic was an expert at *not* staying out of trouble. She said she wanted to lead the federal effort. It took a lot of extra work and ingenuity, but we set a goal of hiring 10,000 people from the welfare rolls within three years and exceeded the goal in less than two. It solidified NPR's reputation as an organization that could do anything, and didn't hurt my reputation either—all because Susan kept me from staying out of trouble.

If you work in government, you'll see things that need doing. You can choose to stay out of trouble, or you can ask yourself, "If not me, who?"

At the other extreme, I once worked for an undersecretary of defense who was concerned that his organization wasn't meeting Pentagon standards of timeliness for answering the mail from Congress, business, and ordinary citizens. He bought a foot-high statue of the monster Godzilla and presented it at his weekly staff meetings to the assistant secretary whose organization had the worst record for that week in answering the mail on time. He was a sensible man and would probably have been shocked had he heard my boss, an assistant secretary, announce that his *number one priority* was to not get the Godzilla. Guess what that did to the priorities of the organization.

4. BE UPLIFTING

At a productivity conference put on by the DOD in 1982, while waiting for the opening session to start, I introduced myself to the person sitting next to me. He was Dave Luther, chief of quality for Corning. I asked him about Corning's approach to productivity.

"Corning's approach is never to use the word 'productivity,'" Dave replied. "Productivity sounds like you're taking something away from people. They won't jump out of bed in the morning and rush to work to improve productivity. We talk about 'quality.' People will lie awake nights trying to figure out how to improve quality."

It was a new idea for me then—the idea that a simple word or phrase could inspire people to lie awake at night trying to figure out how to do their work better. It works at all levels, from huge corporations to midsize government agencies to teams of just a few people. Earlier in this book, I talked about people at Merck giving their all to bring relief to sick people. At the Federal Student Aid Agency, Greg Woods has 6,000 enthusiastic people who "help put America through school." At the U.S. Trademark Office, Jean Logan got her small team to believe they weren't just registering trademarks; they were promoting the economic vitality of American businessmen and businesswomen.

People want purpose in their work. They'll toil grudgingly to cut stone. They'll put their hearts and bodies into building castles.

5. BE POSITIVE

Some people look for things that went wrong and try to fix them. I look for things that went right and try to build on them. I don't mean to minimize mistakes; they have to be dealt with. But the leader has to keep focused on reinforcing success, not on preventing failure. It's like a CEO emphasizing sales growth rather than cost cutting. Both are important, but only one has the potential for unlimited success.

My biggest success at DOD was MIP. In 1984, I had spent months scheming about how to get it started. I planned a months-long campaign that culminated with General Bill Creech offering TAC's Moody Air Force Base as the first model installation. I was ready to relax, having accomplished my goal. Then Ron Susi, an Air Force colonel on my staff, shook me up. "You can't relax now. You just got the most influential general in the country to sign up for your program. Now you have to go all out to make it a success."

It wasn't hard to convince me. I put everybody I could find (NOT just everybody I could spare) to work on model installations. I converted the NATO Programs directorate to MIP directorate. I didn't ask permission, because I would never have gotten it. The effort paid off: MIP became arguably DOD's most effective quality management effort and started to change DOD's whole culture from centralization to decentralization—or from communism to democracy, as I preferred to call it.

Be positive with people. They like it and respond. I once gave Doug Farbrother some feedback on a speech he was writing for Vice President Gore. "Perfect, Doug. I wouldn't change a word."

Doug responded with pleasure. *"That's* my idea of constructive criticism."

When you can't say "perfect," and you must be critical, begin by acknowledging some value in what you're criticizing. If it's somebody's honest effort, it shouldn't be too hard to find something worthwhile to acknowledge.

And say "thank you." It will astonish people. I once wrote a short thank you note to the secretary to the secretary of defense. She walked halfway around the Pentagon (a long way) to thank me and to tell me it was the first time in thirty years of government service that anyone had thanked her for anything.

6. BE ENABLING

Pete Daley was an Air Force officer that I appointed director of environmental policy in OSD. Pete kept coming up with big ideas that made me nervous, and I was forever finding some plausible reason to send him back to the drawing board. Pete was smart enough to start sending his proposals to Doug Farbrother, who was my deputy at the time.

One day Doug sent me Pete's latest proposal with Doug's handwritten note, "Vintage Daley."

I asked Doug what he meant. Doug replied, "Whenever Pete gets an idea, the way to manage him is to slap him on the back and say, 'Way to go, Pete. Go with it.' Pete's enthusiasm will make his good ideas succeed, and his intelligence will let him find out faster than you can which are the bad ideas."

That's how I "managed" Pete from then on and how I "managed" all the talented people I was supposed to manage.

People want to be in charge of their part of the world. When you give them the authority to do their work the way they want to do it, they respond with enthusiasm and creativity, and they produce things you would never dream of.

7. BE CONTROLLING

Putting people in charge of their part of the world does not, however, mean letting them do whatever they want. The leader must guard the core principles of the enterprise—that is, the leader's own core principles.

Thus, Jack Welch of GE and General Bill Creech, both fanatics about decentralizing and delegating authority, said they would fire managers rather than allow them to mistreat their subordinates.

I had to remove a highly innovative and capable manager because I learned he was carrying out my agenda by threatening people. He was violating core principles, and they were nonnegotiable.

One day at DOD, I got a call for help. A woman had submitted a suggestion to management as part of the Defense Logistics Agency's suggestion program, but months had gone by and she still had not received a response. I asked her to send her suggestion to me.

She had proposed that DOD save millions of dollars by replacing the plastic fork and spoon that were packed in military field rations with a spork™— a rather flimsy combination that looked like a spoon with stubby fork tines carved into the tip.

I explained to her that the *Principles of Excellent Installations* called for excellent services for our customers—the members of the military. I asked her to imagine a soldier in battle—cold, wet, and hungry—trying to eat his stew with a spork and accidentally breaking it, with no substitute. Her suggestion would save money, but at the cost of hurting the troops; therefore, I couldn't support it. As much as I believed in delegation and empowerment, I would never empower anybody to violate the principles.

8. BE UNREASONABLE

Absolutely. General Bill Creech was so unreasonable about appearance that he insisted on fresh paint everywhere. When I was touring Creech's home base,

Langley Air Force Base, I was warned, "Keep moving or somebody will slap some paint on you."

Creech's fanaticism made clear to everybody in his 200,000-person command that he was absolutely, unreasonably, committed to excellence. His sidekick, TAC engineer chief Major General Jud Ellis, was so fanatical about taking care of the troops that he personally insisted on decent-sized bars of soap in TAC's base hotels to replace the tiny bars like those supplied at third-rate hotels in the private sector.

Peters and Waterman wrote that top companies were characterized by a "seemingly unjustifiable overcommitment" to customer service.[2] I loved to use General Ellis's soap bar as an example of seemingly unjustifiable overcommitment in the military.

Creech's emphasis on customer service had an unexpected consequence a couple of years later. Cannon Air Force Base, a TAC base, was a finalist for the Commander in Chief's Award for Best Base in the Air Force, and the team of judges, headed by a major general, was interviewing people on the base. When they came to the base finance office, they began to interview an airman whose job was to reimburse Air Force people for their business travel expenses. In the middle of the interview, a sergeant came to the service window.

"Excuse me, sirs, I have a customer," the airman said, and turned her back on the general and two colonels to wait on the sergeant. Her commitment to customer service was enough to tip the balance and win the top award for Cannon.

George Bernard Shaw wrote, "The reasonable man adapts himself to the world; the unreasonable one persists in trying to adapt the world to himself. Therefore all progress depends on the unreasonable man."[3]

9. BE CLEAR

I wrote in chapter 4 about how I was inspired by the story of Rene McPherson, then CEO of Dana Corporation, who had thrown out Dana's twenty-two-inch-thick stack of policy manuals and replaced them with a one-page statement of philosophy.[4] I decided to do the same thing in DOD and soon produced the one-page *Principles of Excellent Installations*. I sent a copy to McPherson with a note saying he had inspired me to emulate his Dana experience at the Pentagon.

McPherson wrote back to congratulate me and to say how important it was to be clear with people about what you expect from them. Once you're clear about that, they'll know best how to do their jobs.

But clarity of message doesn't count for much if people don't get the message. I was moderating a panel on the role of the leader at the first Global Forum on Reinventing Government, when one of the panelists, EPA administrator Carol Browner, made a casual comment that the leader had to make her purpose clear.

"How do you do that?" I asked. "Do you just tell people in a memo or a directive what your purpose is?"

"Oh, no, no! You have to tell them and tell them, every day, everywhere you go, and repeat it until it starts to make you nauseous. Not until then can you assume that your message has even started to get through."

When you're perfectly clear and the message has gotten through, wonderful things start to happen.

One of the best days of my career was when I got to turn down the Navy auditors' request for help in getting Dick McSeveny to accept "minimum acceptable" as a standard for Marine barracks. (See chapter 13.) McSeveny held out for excellence because the message—the Principles of Excellent Installations—had gotten through. His commitment to the principles was an important factor in improving quality of life for Marines.

10. THINK THREE

Clarity and repetition aren't enough if the message is too complicated to remember. Most people have a hard time remembering more than three things. Certainly I can't.

The Bible says that the Lord requires of man only three things: "To do justice, and to love kindness, and to walk humbly with your God."[5] West Point's values are Duty, Honor, Country. The three rules of real estate value are location, location, and location.

When I became deputy assistant secretary of defense for Installations, I quickly developed a three-part agenda that I repeated over and over until it was widely understood across the defense establishment.

1. Improve working and living conditions for the military.
2. Improve the efficiency of base operations.
3. Take care of our troops overseas without provoking Congress. (A lot of U.S. construction money was going overseas rather than to their districts.)

When I first met with Gore, I told him my three rules for changing huge organizations, and he embraced them.

1. Have a simple uplifting message that you repeat over and over.
2. Use colorful stories in plain English, with props, to make your aims clear.
3. Praise and reward people who are doing what you want, and don't waste one minute looking for fraud, waste, or abuse.

The rule of three is flexible. This chapter lists ten lessons, but it's easy to re-arrange them into three. For example:

1. For you: be pleasant, be trusting, be bold.
2. For others: be uplifting, be positive, be enabling.
3. For your principles: be controlling, be unreasonable, be clear.

Notice I didn't need to include "think three"—it's there by example.

Three things are easy to remember. A dean was describing the new curriculum to a reception celebrating the grand opening of a major American college of public administration. "There are four tracks," he started. I smelled trouble. "The policy track, the management track, the finance track, and, uh, uh, uh, the fourth track." Stick to three things.

NOTES

1. Francis Fukuyama, *Trust: The Social Virtues and the Creation of Prosperity* (New York: Free Press, 1995).

2. Thomas J. Peters and Robert H. Waterman, Jr., *In Search of Excellence* (New York: Harper & Row, 1982).

3. George Bernard Shaw, *Man and Superman* (New York: Brentano's, 1905).

4. Peters and Waterman, *In Search of Excellence.*

5. Revised Standard Version, Micah 6:8.

Ciao, Mommy.
That Means Goodbye

I never did any career planning. After leaving MIT, I worked for two years at Cities Service Oil Company (now Citgo) and left because I was bored. I then worked for the nuclear division of North American Aviation (now Rockwell), and left there, too, out of boredom. Then I joined Garrett-AiResearch, a developer of high-tech heat exchangers and power systems for the aerospace industry (now merged and remerged into Honeywell).

I was in my element as a heat transfer engineer at Garrett and assumed I would never leave there. Then I got an intriguing invitation to come interview at the Pentagon. I took that job as a senior analyst in OSD, and I expected to remain there until Larry Korb twisted my arm to take the job as deputy assistant secretary of defense for Installations. There, too, I expected to serve forever.

Even when I was scheming to become a part of the reinventing government effort in 1993, I expected to do it at the Pentagon, where my heart was with the frontline workers and the troops.

My work at Installations left a mental image with me to this day that drove me to reinvent. It was a couple of airmen trying to scrub tire marks off bright yellow tape that marked a path for forklifts and tractors (which towed aircraft) to follow inside the maintenance hangers at Moody Air Force Base, the first model installation.

The Air Force culture is admirably one of extraordinary cleanliness, especially on floors and pavements used by aircraft, because foreign objects can destroy an aircraft if they get into the engine. Floors of Air Force hangars sparkle.

Sadly, however, a well-meaning but misguided safety rule of OSD required that all hangar areas used by vehicles be delineated with bright yellow tape. Every time an aircraft was towed into the hangar, its tires left wide black marks on the yellow tape. The black marks meant the floors didn't sparkle. That's why when I visited Moody, I met airmen scrubbing and scrubbing, trying to get the black tire marks off OSD-imposed yellow tape.

MIP freed the Moody airmen, but it didn't end all the craziness that headquarters imposed on people in the field. I was quite happy to stay at DOD to keep fighting that battle.

Then Gore made me project director of the NPR, where I learned that every government agency had its own version of scrubbing the yellow tape, sapping the energy from workers who were capable of greatness. I decided that my most important work was to be "energizer-in-chief," and I put that title on my business card. There was plenty to do, and even though we accomplished much, much remained to be done.

By 1998, I had worked for Gore for six years and fully expected to do it longer. I assumed that in 2001 *President* Gore would call me to reinvent some important agency awash in (metaphorical) yellow tape.

But one day that fall, Roxane, my wife, returned from a trip to visit Alexandra Stern, our two-year-old granddaughter, and her parents in California. Roxane told me how she had taught Alexandra to say "ciao." A few minutes later, Roxane and Alex were about to go for a walk when Alex ran in to tell her mother, "Ciao, Mommy. That means goodbye."

Roxane was bursting with joy as she recounted this little story, and her joy filled me, too. The joy was available to us (multiplied by three for the three grandchildren we had, Jeffrey Thomson, Alexandra, and Ethan Le—and now by five with Derek Le's and Jack Stern's births in 2001) a couple of times a year as long as we lived in the Washington, D.C., area. Or it was something we could share in all the time if we lived near our grandchildren. Finally, it was time to do career planning.

Unlike my past jobs, the NPR job was one I knew I couldn't keep forever. NPR was a temporary organization, and would almost certainly disappear after the election, no matter who won. I loved the mission and the people, but I was ready for a new challenge.

I had been watching for the opportunity to implement my ideas about decentralization, deregulation, and excellence on a larger scale. Back in 1995 the position of IG of the Defense Department had become vacant. *There* was an opportunity—I could transform the IG from a relentless defender of the status quo to a force for common sense, innovation, and excellence. Elaine Kamarck thought it was a great idea, and called DOD Deputy Secretary John Deutsch to urge him to appoint me. Deutsch objected, saying that the job needed a "cop." Elaine argued that was just what defense *didn't* need. They already *had* plenty of cops; what they needed was a reinventor. But Deutsch was unconvinced, and I stayed at NPR.

Over time I decided there were just two dream jobs for me. As deputy secretary of defense I could transform the biggest department in government, one that still stirred my blood. Or as commissioner of the Immigration and Naturalization Service I could make a difference to millions of immigrants who were treated wretchedly by INS. I believed in America as a nation of immigrants, the place that gave, and still gives, unlimited opportunities to millions yearning to breathe free, just as it had for my grandparents over a hundred years ago.

I didn't know whether I had a realistic shot at either of my dream jobs if Gore was elected. But one thing I knew for sure—our grandchildren were growing up. Jeffrey was five, Alexandra three, and Ethan one. They were changing every day. Roxane and I could be on hand to be a part of that. Or not. There wouldn't be another chance to share the joy of their growing up, learning to say ciao and a million other little wonders that we would miss by not being nearby.

It was time for us to leave Washington. My government career was over. I had entered government service without a clue about what it would be like. I left it with 1,001 lessons—a story behind every one.

My final act as a government worker was to write a farewell letter to all the reinventors I was leaving.

May 19, 1999

Today is my last as a federal employee, after thirty years of service. From the first day, back in the bowels of the Pentagon in 1969, to my last assignment leading the vice president's campaign to reinvent government, it's been " . . . one of those fabulous flings, a trip to the moon on gossamer wings." My jobs have been so rewarding and so fun (most days) that I never ceased to marvel that they'd actually pay me to do this.

I received many honors and much praise at my going away party, but the honor I'll always keep in my heart is hearing Vice President Gore say, "Do you know who knew what was wrong in government and how to fix it? Frontline employees. They are the ones who knew—who still know—and Bob became their voice inside this White House."

If I was the voice of frontline employees inside the White House, then my time was well spent indeed. Now here's a serious question for all you reinventors. What will you do for energy after the Energizer-in-Chief is gone? I'll tell you what to do.

Go back to the roots of reinvention. Listen to the GS-9 benefits clerk in Sacramento who is trying to help people get the benefits they have coming—but who isn't trusted to approve a disability claim delivered in person by a recent amputee. She will give you energy to keep reinventing.

Go back to the roots of reinvention—to the GS-14 program manager who's creating decent housing for the poor—but who gets hassled over timecards and needs a dozen approval signatures on a simple answer to a routine Congressional letter. He'll re-energize you any time you need it.

Go to the roots of reinvention, and listen to all the men and women who signed up to make a difference for America—listen to their stories about working like Dilbert in dreary cubicles, contending with pointy-haired bosses who don't have a clue about trust and enthusiasm. Go get in touch with the power in them—the untapped potential that, unleashed, will restore America's faith in government.

I was lucky enough to get in touch with that power long ago, and it energized me for decades—filled me with enough energy to spare for so many of you.

But, now the Energizer-in-Chief has gone. You're going to have to go to the source yourselves—to the men and women of government.

They will tell you the job of reinvention is not done. They will tell you how to do it. And they will give you the energy to go on.

As for me, my grandchildren are calling. They're in California doing all sorts of things for the first time—while here, I have done more and more for the last time. All in all, it's time for me to be with them.

But I'll never forget any of you—or the dream we share.

And I'll be out there with the rest of America watching—not settling for any less than the best—Americans never settle for less.

So, someday when you're down—when a setback makes you wonder what's the use—just remember my pink ears, my cotton tail—and keep on going, and going, and going, and going.

Bob Stone

Appendix

Principles of
Excellent Installations

Principles of
EXCELLENT INSTALLATIONS

These principles guide all members of the Excellent Installations Team.

Purpose

To provide for our customers-the soldiers, sailors, marines, and airmen who defend America—excellent places to work and live, and excellent base services.

Serve Our Customers

We are here only to serve our customers and their families.

Know our customers and their desires.

Get out and talk and listen to them in their workplaces, homes, and communities.

Tell the American people, the Congress, and our bosses, what our customers need, using real-life stories that people can relate to.

Show unjustifiable overcommitment to improving facilities and services for our customers.

Manage for Excellence

The hundreds of thousands of people—in and out of uniform—who work at Defense installations are our most important asset.

Provide them with freedom and incentives to unleash their drive and entrepreneurial genius.

Discourage conformity, uniformity, and centralization because they stifle innovation.

Push responsibility and authority as far down into the organization as possible—and that's a lot further than most people think.

Promote competition by providing installations people lots of information on how people at other installations are doing at similar jobs, then celebrate the winners.

Encourage installation commanders to take charge, use all the authority available to them, demand relief from stifling over-regulation, and exercise an innovative spirit.

Pay for Excellence

Defense cannot afford less than excellence. There is no such thing as a bad investment in excellent facilities for our people, because excellent facilities engender pride—the fuel of human accomplishment.

Protect our installations from deterioration. Every year replace at least 2% of our physical plant, and do more repair and maintenance than the year before.

Encourage and enable the troops to improve their own facilities. They get better facilities far sooner and a greater feeling of pride and ownership.

Foster the Excellent Installation Approach

Keep fighting the natural tendency of large organizations to ration authority, to over-centralize, and to over-regulate.

Help anyone who is trying to promote the excellent installation idea.

Find examples of what the excellent installation approach has accomplished and hold them up as models for others.

EXCELLENT INSTALLATIONS — THE FOUNDATION OF DEFENSE

Index

About the Author

Bob Stone was born and raised in Delaware and educated as a chemical engineer at MIT. He spent eleven years practicing engineering in the private sector, then twenty-four years at the Pentagon, where he started a quality revolution, improved the standard of living for military men and women, and became widely recognized as one of the top public sector managers in America. He then spent six years as Al Gore's right-hand man in his campaign to spread customer service, empowerment, and trust throughout the U.S. government.

Bob is a partner in the Public Strategies Group, Inc., America's leading consultancy specializing in reinventing government. He lives with his wife, Roxane Stern, in Los Angeles, where they spend lots of time with their five grandchildren when he's not consulting and lecturing on reinvention and leadership. His e-mail is bob@psgrp.com.